Architecture of t...

Andreas Volwahsen
Henri Stierlin (Ed.)

Islamic India

Photos: Andreas Volwahsen

Benedikt Taschen

Editor of Series   Henri Stierlin
Plans   Andreas Volwahsen and Gerd Mader

Contents

Introduction

The western world is exposed to a steady flood of information about India. On the one hand we hear of famines and mendicant monks, and on the other of vast wealth and an impressive modern film industry. To comprehend these apparent contradictions it may be helpful to consider in detail the country's historical background. Only then can we understand the social structure and culture of a land as fettered by tradition as India.

Interest in Indian culture is generally concentrated on Buddhist and Hindu literature and art. Their architectural achievements are in contrast sadly neglected.

This volume deals with a certain period in the history of Indian architecture: with the buildings erected during the reigns of the Islamic sultans and emperors who ruled over the peoples of the subcontinent between the tenth and nineteenth centuries. None of these rulers was an Indian. Their religion differed from that of native Hindus; they dressed differently from them and spoke a foreign tongue. Most of the natives regarded this alien rule as a burdensome yoke.

The architecture of the Indo-Islamic rulers originated in Persia. It can usually be distinguished without difficulty from Buddhist and Hindu religious architecture, the subject of a separate volume in this series.

We shall be particularly concerned here with the fusion that took place between Islamic and Hindu architectural concepts, since this helps to explain the various stages through which the Indo-Islamic style passed in the course of its evolution.

The centres in which the Muslim architects operated are situated in Northern India, which from the sixteenth century onwards was ruled by the Mughuls, descendants of Chingiz Khan. They built innumerable castles and tombs of red sandstone and white marble. Shah Jahan, the Great Mughul, erected for his dead queen and favourite wife one of the most

3

splendid monuments in the Orient – the Taj Mahal at Agra. This building and many others of note will be discussed here, not as tourist attractions – as symbols of a fairytale world of 'One Thousand and One Nights' – but as outstanding examples of design and technical perfection, hardly inferior to works in the West.

We shall examine not only the spectacular architecture of the Mughuls but also that of earlier sultanates in Northern India and that of the Islamic empires in Southern India. This survey does not aspire to give a comprehensive picture of Indo-Islamic architecture, but, despite the limited space available, we shall endeavour to present some new analyses of the structure of several of these monuments, to discuss certain features in detail, and to describe the most important sites.

In designing all their buildings the Hindus took theology into account. Because their temples were built largely in stone, it is these that have in the main survived. Muslim monuments, however, were designed without any thought of a transcendental significance. We find some purely functional or decorative secular buildings; palaces display the same courtly features as mosques. It is possible to understand these architectural forms without having to inquire deeply into Islam, the religion of the men who built them.

Even today it is only with some hesitation that historians of architecture study cultures outside the classical Mediterranean world. We shall attempt to demonstrate that a relatively little explored area such as Indo-Islamic architecture has as much to offer the student as Egypt, Greece or Rome.

Since the reader will no doubt be less familiar with the historical background of Indo-Islamic culture, we shall summarize in brief the history of Islamic rule in India before discussing the monuments themselves.

1. Historical Summary

Already a few years after the death of the Prophet Muhammad (Mohammed; 570–632), under the leadership of the Caliphs, the Prophet's successors, the peoples of the Arabian desert began to expand the theocratic empire of Islam.

The Ghaznavids

In the tenth century the Muslim advance eastwards reached the area of what is today Afghanistan. At Ghazni a Turkish dynasty was established. Sabuktigin of Ghazni (977–997) pressed on into India and, after defeating the armies of the Hindu kings, fixed the Indus as the eastern frontier of his empire. For the next eight centuries the political and cultural history of Northern India was to be determined by Islamic rulers.

At the beginning of the second millennium A.D. Sabuktigin's son, Mahmud of Ghazni, repeatedly invaded the fertile plains of Northern India, and each time withdrew to his own territory laden with treasure and followed by an army of Indian slaves. The more peaceful policy of the succeeding Ghaznavids permitted Prince Muhammad of Ghur to expel this dynasty in 1173, whereupon he likewise began to launch raids into India. After an initial failure, at the end of the twelfth century he advanced as far as Delhi. One of his generals reached Nalanda, the ancient Buddhist university town in the Bihar district; another, a former slave named Qutb-ud-din Aibak, occupied Benares.

Slave dynasty

When Muhammad of Ghur was murdered on the Indus in 1206 his officers nominated Qutb-ud-din Aibak to be their commander-in-chief. As the first independent Muslim ruler in India, he assumed the title of Sultan of Delhi. After a four-year reign he died as the result of an accident while playing polo, and was succeeded by his son-in-law, Iltutmish. While the Sultans of Delhi were still preoccupied with consolidating their power, the subcontinent was threatened with invasion by the Mongols, who had already laid waste the

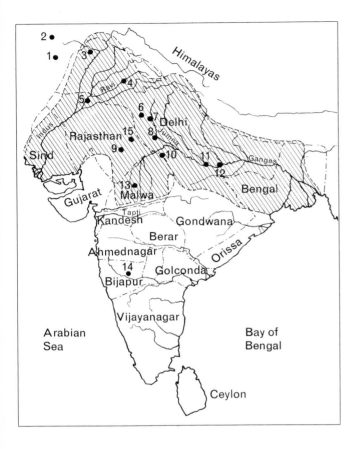

The dynasty founded by Qutb-ud-din Aibak (1206–1290 A.D.) is known as the Slave Dynasty, because the sultans were usually former slaves who, time and again, were overthrown and superseded by their favourites. After Iltutmish's death attempts were indeed made to introduce a regular system of succession, but Iltutmish's daughter was immediately deposed by her slaves. After various members of the ruling family had tried in vain to assert control, one of Iltutmish's sons succeeded in maintaining himself in office, but only because sovereignty was for all practical purposes exercised by his slave and father-in-law, Balban. During his reign, too, the pattern of slave revolts threatened to continue, but Balban managed to control and curb potential rebels by measures of extreme cruelty. He was followed by his depraved grandson, who was murdered in 1290 shortly after he succeeded, and the rebel Jalal-ud-din then usurped the throne. He too ruled for no more than a few years, and was murdered by his son-in-law, Ala-ud-din, who appraised the situation realistically and ruled purely by terror, on a scale that soon exceeded that of Balban. In 1316, however, a plot was successfully engineered by the slave Kafur, who had risen to the rank of general while in the sultan's service, but shortly afterwards he too was put to death. Ala-ud-din's son ascended the throne, and likewise fell victim to one of his favourites.

Tughluq dynasty

In 1320 Ghiyas-ud-din Tughluq took over the government. This marked the beginning of a relatively peaceful era in which the administration and economy could recover from the ill effects of the struggles for power and rule of terror of the thirteenth century. When the ruler and his favourite son were finally killed by a collapsing pavilion, it was thought to have been no accident, but the work of Muhammad bin Tughluq, who now came to power in his father's place.

A description of Muhammad bin Tughluq is to be found in the account left by Ibn Batuta:
'Muhammad keeps his subjects in suspense by two

\\\\\\\\\ Expansion of Sultanate of Delhi during reign of Iltutmish (1210–1236)

— - — --Political divisions in India on the eve of Babur's invasion (1526)

1 Ghazni	6 Panipat	11 Allahbad
2 Kabul	7 Delhi (Shahjahanabad)	12 Benares
3 Peshawar	8 Agra (Akharabad)	13 Ujjain
4 Lahore	9 Ajmer	14 Bijapur
5 Multan	10 Gwalior	15 Jaipur

Punjab during the reign of Chingiz Khan. Unexpectedly, however, Delhi was spared a barbarian assault, for the Mongol hordes withdrew to the north-west.

methods in particular: by gifts and bloodshed. In front of his palace one may see several impoverished people on their way to acquiring wealth, or the bodies of several persons who have just been put to death. Tales are widespread of his generosity and courage, of his cruelty and harshness.'

In the middle of the fourteenth century the army raised Firuz Shah to the throne. About his love of architecture the Shah writes in his autobiography: 'Among the many gifts which God has bestowed upon me, His humble servant, was a desire to erect public buildings. So I built many mosques and colleges and monasteries that the learned and the elders, the devout and the holy, might worship God in these edifices, and aid the kind builder with their prayers[1].' Firuz Shah was succeeded by several weak sultans.

At the end of the fourteenth century Mongol armies under Timur crossed the passes which gave access to the subcontinent from Central Asia. They conquered Delhi and extensive areas of Northern India. The empire of the Turkish sultans was broken up. But this time, too, the Mongols withdrew from India, because their armies were needed to resist rebellions in western Asia. The provinces of their empire declared themselves independent.

From 1414 onwards Delhi was governed by the Sayyids, who had been put in office by Timur; in 1450 they were succeeded by Afghan rulers belonging to the Lodi tribe. In 1526 the last Lodi ruler was killed in battle against King Babur, who invaded India from Afghanistan.

Mughul Emperors

Babur, a descendant of Timur and Chingiz Khan, became king of Ferghana at the age of twelve. His greatest ambition was to reconquer the vast empire which had been ruled by his grandfather, Timur. He began by taking Samarkand, but during his absence the capital Andijan fell into the hands of his rivals. He lost his empire, then regained it; finally, after conducting several campaigns with varying success,

he had to renounce both Ferghana and the land which had been Timur's. With only 10,000 followers he gained a footing in Kabul and then moved on to India in search of a new kingdom. At Panipat he defeated 50,000 men and 1,000 elephants of the sultan of Delhi, aided by the use of firearms, which were hitherto unknown in India.

The 'master and conqueror of the mighty empire of Hindustan' notes despondently in his memoirs: 'Hindustan is a country of few charms. Its people have no good looks; of social intercourse, paying and receiving visits there is none; of genius and capacity none; in handicraft and work there is no form or symmetry, method or quality... Their residences have no charm, air, regularity or symmetry. The chief advantage of Hindustan lies in its size and its riches of gold and silver[2].'

Babur's criticism of certain characteristics of the Hindu mentality and society is no doubt exaggerated, but it shows that he, although a descendant of one of the most barbarous tribes in Central Asia, grew up under the influence of the advanced culture of Persia. He was not only a distinguished general but also one of the finest poets of his time and the most reliable historian of the empire.

Babur was frequently referred to by contemporaries as 'the Great Mughul' (Persian word for Mongol); his dynasty was accordingly called that of the Great Mughuls.

Humayun

In 1530 Humayun, a less ambitious ruler, succeeded to the throne. He was not recognized by Sher Khan, Babur's governor in Bihar, and after suffering defeat in two battles was expelled to Persia, where he lived in exile at the court of the Persian Shah.

Sher Khan, who now adopted the imperial name of Sher Shah, was an outstanding administrator who did much to reform the fiscal system. He also promoted many projects for public buildings, such as rest houses and hospitals. His successors ruled for only a short time, because in 1555 Humayun reconquered his empire with the aid of a Persian army. In the following year the emperor fell down the stairs of his library and died. Outside Delhi his wife erected one of the finest of the Mughul tombs in his honour. General Himu, a Hindu, took advantage of the absence of the thirteen-year-old heir to the throne, Akbar, to have himself acclaimed in Delhi as ruler of a Hindu empire. He took the title of 'Raja' and mobilized Hindu troops against Akbar when the latter returned from Kabul. Himu's army was, however, defeated; he himself was taken prisoner and executed.

Akbar

Akbar first placed himself under the guardianship of his tutor, Bairam Khan; but at the age of eighteen he decided to take the affairs of state in hand personally. Bairam Khan rebelled against him, but was captured, pardoned and sent on a pilgrimage to Mecca.

Of all Islamic rulers in India Akbar is the most interesting and eccentric. Since he was also the greatest builder of them all, we shall discuss his life and times in greater detail. He appears to have been a bold commander, fully occupied in suppressing revolutions in the provinces or palace revolts, and in undertaking wars of conquest.

Akbar was also an obstinate mystic who, although educated as an orthodox Muslim, developed a creed of his own, the Din-i-Ilahi. Father Monserat S.J., who lived at the imperial court for several years, records: 'He was well versed in the laws of many religious communities, to the study of which he had dedicated himself with particular care. Although he could neither read nor write, he enjoyed discussions with men of learning, and of these there were at his court always a dozen or more, who debated in his presence the most diverse problems. He listened to their discussions, secretly hoping to be able to overcome his lack of education. Basically he was of melancholic disposition and suffered from epilepsy. As a diversion he sought refuge in pleasures such as fights between

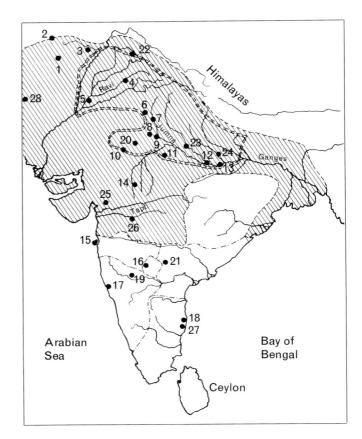

‗‗‗‗ Akbar's empire in year of his accession

\\\\\\\\\\\\ Mughul Empire during reign of Akbar (1556–1605)

1 Ghazni	10 Ajmer	20 Jaipur
2 Kabul	11 Gwalior	21 Hyderabad
3 Peshawar	12 Allahbad	22 Srinagar
4 Lahore	13 Benares	23 Kanauj
5 Multan	14 Ujjain	24 Jaunpur
6 Panipat	15 Bombay	25 Champanir
7 Delhi	16 Gulbarga	26 Burhanpur
(Shahjahanabad)	17 Goa	27 Mahaballipuram
8 Fathepur Sikri	18 Madras	28 Kandahar
9 Agra (Akharabad)	19 Bijapur	

elephants, camels, buffaloes, rams and cocks, or else had gladiators perform their art in Roman fashion, or fencers duel until one of them was slain.'

During his campaigns he once had 30,000 enemy peasants and mercenaries massacred to no purpose; on another occasion he watched with great delight a slaughter he had arranged between hostile yogis and sanyasis, reinforcing the weaker party with his own troops so that the two sides in this bloody spectacle should fight on equal terms.

Later the emperor turned to Jainism, which taught that not even the basest living thing might be harmed. He restricted his consumption of meat to a minimum. For nights on end he would sit with a poet who read to him from the sacred books of the Brahmins, Christians, Jews and Muslims. His library became one of the largest in the Orient. Jesuits from the Portuguese commercial settlement at Goa, whom from 1580 onwards he invited to his theological discussions, already saw in him a convert to Christianity. They were bitterly disappointed when in 1582 the learned but wilful monarch proclaimed his own vaguely defined and eclectic creed.

A contemporary remarked:
'From his earliest childhood to his manhood, and from his manhood to old age His Majesty has passed through the most various phases, and through all sorts of religious practices and sectarian beliefs, and has collected everything which people can find in books, with a talent of selection peculiar to him and a spirit of enquiry opposed to every [Islamic] principle. Thus a faith based on some elementary principles traced itself on the mirror of his heart, and, as the result of all the influences which were brought to bear on His Majesty there grew, gradually, ... the conviction in his heart that there were sensible men in all religions and abstemious thinkers and men endowed with miraculous powers among all nations. If some true knowledge were thus confined to one religion, or to a creed like Islam, which was comparatively new, and scarcely a thousand years old, why should one sect assert what another denies, and why should one claim a preference without having superiority conferred upon itself[3]?'

As the first and only interpreter of the new doctrine, Akbar rejected every form of priesthood. Mohammedan prayers were replaced by invocations of the deity couched in general terms. From Hinduism he adopted the idea of the migration of souls, thus contradicting Islamic doctrine on the matter of resurrection. From the Parsees, followers of the prophet Zoroaster who had made their way to India, he took over the worship of fire and the sun. The keynote of his creed was contained in the thesis: 'There is but one God, creator of the universe, who is represented on earth by Akbar'.

In 1579 the emperor in person set foot in the pulpit of the Fathepur Sikri mosque. Overwhelmed by the enormity of this step, he began to tremble and stammer, and then descended from the pulpit.

Eventually, since Akbar did not shrink from bribery and coercion, eighteen prominent persons at court professed the Din-i-Ilahi or 'divine faith'. But, after the death of 'the king of Islam, the asylum of mankind, the commander-in-chief of believers, the shadow of God on earth, Abu-'l-Fath Jalal-ud-din Muhammad Akbar, Padshah-i-Ghazi (whose realm may God preserve for ever more!)', his subjects forgot all about his theological speculations. However, in discussing the cities, palaces and mosques which he built, it is helpful to consider briefly Akbar's ideas. In the monuments he erected we find a blend of Hindu and Islamic elements. The spiritual tension from which the ruler suffered is demonstrated in their eclectic style more clearly than it is in the written testimonies of his 'divine faith'.

In his search for a 'divine language' the emperor hit upon the idea of keeping a number of infants in confinement where they came into contact only with nurses and tutors who were deaf and dumb. When these children were freed after his death, they not surprisingly turned out to be dumb themselves.

More beneficial than Akbar's attempts to discover a 'divine faith' and a 'divine language' were his administrative reforms, to which he gave personal attention for several years. With the aid of Hindu and Muslim ministers he tightened up the judicial system, promoted an atmosphere of tolerance in matters of religion, and abolished unjust fiscal levies. Thus, for example, he introduced a system of taxing the agricultural population according to the amount they produced, instead of assessing villages at a flat rate.

Before Akbar launched his wars of conquest, the Mughul empire had been confined to the Punjab and the plains of the Ganges and Jumna. It was not until his reign that the Rajputana kings were conquered and Gujarat, Malwa, Bihar, Bengal and Orissa annexed. In the south the imperial troops advanced as far as the frontiers of the sultanate of Golconda, while in the north Afghanistan fell to the emperor on the death of the king of Kabul, a brother of Akbar. Within four decades Akbar had welded the sultanates of northern and central India into an empire the size of Europe.

Jahangir

To Akbar's consternation his two sons proved to be alcoholics. Scheming courtiers had already considered setting up as successor one of his grandsons, but when one of his sons died from the effects of drink, Akbar decided that the other, Prince Salim, should inherit the empire. In 1605 Salim succeeded to the throne, assuming the title of Jahangir-Nur-ud-din ('world-seizer', 'light of the faith'). As the consequences of his intemperance became ever more apparent, he tended more and more to leave matters of state to Nur Mahal ('light of the palace'). 'I need no more than a quart of wine and a pound of meat'—this was his motto.

Nur Mahal was the daughter of a Persian adventurer who had come to Akbar's court at the instigation of her family. Jahangir, then still Prince Salim, wanted her as his bride, but this was prevented by Akbar, who married her off to an Afghan nobleman instead. After Akbar's death Jahangir had no compunction about having this Afghan put to death and

had Nur Mahal brought to his court. Finally she consented to become his wife. As a sign of gratitude the emperor made her father, I'timad-ud-daula, Lord High Treasurer and Wazir of the empire.

Nur Mahal—an imperial decree ordained that she was to be known only as Nur Jahan, or 'light of the world'—built for her father near Agra a tomb in white marble. As we shall see, this mausoleum was a turning-point in Mughul architecture.

Jahangir showed little interest in architecture, although he completed Akbar's tomb at Sikandra near Agra without stinting the high cost of the fine materials used. His special concern was reserved for painting. It was under his patronage that the best miniatures in Indo-Islamic style were executed. Although orthodox Muslims are forbidden to depict human beings and animals, under Jahangir artists were encouraged to paint such subjects.

Shah Jahan

The death of Jahangir was followed by a struggle for the succession. Prince Khusru, who had repeatedly instigated rebellions against Jahangir, had already been blinded by his father. The rightful heir, Shah Jahan, was threatened only by his nephews. As a precautionary measure he had them all assassinated. Nur Jahan was thus the sole survivor of the imperial family, apart from the emperor, who ruled from 1628 onwards as the fourth Great Mughul. Although his mother was a Hindu, his domestic policy was in no way characterized by a tolerant approach toward all religious groups. On the contrary, he nourished hatred in equal measure for Hindus and Christians—especially the latter, since the Portuguese had supported his father during one of the rebellions he had raised. In 1632 imperial troops burned down the Portuguese settlement at Hooghly; only a few of the inhabitants succeeded in escaping to the safety of their ships. Four hundred captive Portuguese were taken to Agra, where a few decades earlier their compatriots had been welcomed by the monarch as honoured guests.

The humiliation of the Hindus began with the destruction of many temples and the promulgation of a law prohibiting the renovation of old temples or the building of new ones. Intermarriage between Hindus and Muslims was also forbidden. To give a visible sign of their religious affiliation Hindus were ordered to fasten their upper garment on the left according to Hindu custom. Iconoclasm led many Hindus to become converted, some of them voluntarily and others under pressure.

In 1630, while Shah Jahan was pushing ahead with the conquest of the south, his favourite wife, Mumtaz Mahal, a granddaughter of I'timad-ud-daula, died. She had been his constant companion on his campaigns in the south, and he had entrusted her with many affairs of state. Her death plunged him into such despair that he refused for a week to take any food or to carry out any governmental function. He ordered two years of deep mourning at court. Festivals and musical entertainments were forbidden, as was the wearing of jewellery or the use of perfume. The emperor even thought of retiring and dividing among his sons an empire which now extended from Afghanistan to the tributary sultanate of Bijapur.

When Shah Jahan became seriously ill – apparently as a result of debauchery in the harem – people expected his favourite son Dara to mount the throne. His brothers in the provincial cities had other ideas, for each of them was determined to seize power for himself. They led their armies against Delhi. From the battles that were fought between them Aurangzib emerged the victor. He outwitted his ailing father and had him arrested. Shah Jahan spent the last four years of his life as a prisoner in the gilded marble palace within the fort at Agra, and from there he could see, on a bend in the river, the Taj Mahal – the shimmering white mausoleum in which his favourite wife was buried.

Tavernier, a French traveller who lived at the court of the Great Mughul, wrote:
'It is a most surprising thing, however, that not one of the servants of this great emperor offered to assist

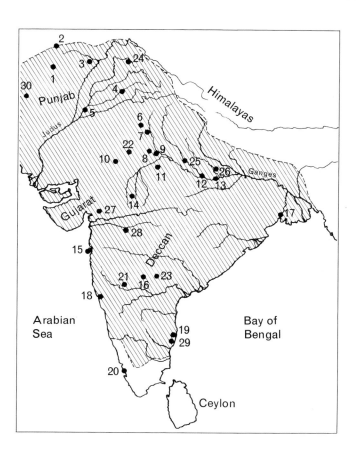

\\\\\\\\\\ Mughul Empire under Aurangzib, late 17th century

1 Ghazni	10 Ajmer	21 Bijapur
2 Kabul	11 Gwalior	22 Jaipur
3 Peshawar	12 Allahabad	23 Hyderabad
4 Lahore	13 Benares	24 Srinagar
5 Multan	14 Ujjain	25 Kanauj
6 Panipat	15 Bombay	26 Jaunpur
7 Delhi	16 Gulbarga	27 Champanir
(Shahjahanabad)	17 Calcutta	28 Burhanpur
8 Fathepur Sikri	18 Goa	29 Mahaballipuram
9 Agra	19 Madras	30 Kandahar
(Akharabad)	20 Cochin	

him; that all his subjects abandoned him, and that they turned their eyes to the rising sun, recognizing no one as emperor but Aurangzib–Shah Jahan, although still living, having passed from their memories. If perchance there were any who felt touched by his misfortunes, fear made them silent and caused them basely to abandon an emperor who had governed them like a father, and with a mildness which is not common with sovereigns. For although he was severe enough to the nobles when they failed to perform their duties, he arranged all things for the comfort of the people, by whom he was so much beloved, though they gave no signs of it at this crisis[4].'

Aurangzib

Prince Dara made several further attempts to seize power but was betrayed and executed by Aurangzib. Like his father before him, Aurangzib had all the heirs to the throne disposed of, to ensure his own security. This ruler, who in matters of state and military strategy was extremely cautious, committed great follies in his religious policy. Bigoted Sunnites in the cabinet supported him in adopting an intolerant attitude toward the Hindus. As in the reign of Shah Jahan, temples were pulled down and Hindus discriminated against. The emperor weakened his own power by attempting to exclude all Hindus from the administration. At court music and dancing were forbidden. Distinguished painters and architects who had served Shah Jahan were dismissed.

Aurangzib succeeded in finally subjugating Bijapur, Golconda and almost the whole of Southern India, but at the same time the first signs of collapse were already visible in the administration and economic life of his vast domains. It seemed to be impossible to hold together an empire extending from Kabul to Madras and containing so many disparate peoples, languages and religions. In Rajasthan the Rajputs rose to power; on the west coast the Maratha empire crystallized out of a national Hindu movement for independence.

The emperor spent most of his time in the south, where his troops were worn down by guerilla warfare. Meanwhile Mughul power crumbled in the north. In 1707 Aurangzib died at the age of 88, and the usual struggle for the succession began.

Disintegration of the Mughul empire

After Bahadur Shah, Aurangzib's eldest son, had his two brothers executed, he managed to win the upper hand in the succession struggle. Bahadur Shah was then followed by Jahandar Shah and Farrukhsiyar, both of whom were assassinated. Muhammad Shah, who reigned from 1719 to 1748, was a weak monarch. One of his ministers withdrew to Hyderabad, where he ruled independently as Nizam-ul-mulk; one of his generals likewise took advantage of the confused situation to found the kingdom of Oudh. Encouraged by this political and military weakness the Persian emperor Nadir Shah invaded India with a large army by way of Kabul and Lahore. The Mughul emperor was unable to grasp the fact that his empire was disintegrating. At Delhi drinking bouts and festivities continued. The capital surrendered without offering any resistance and Nadir Shah moved into the palace as an unwelcome guest of the Mughul emperor. When some Hindus took up arms, after a ridiculous quarrel with Persian soldiers, Nadir Shah gave orders to massacre the entire population.

Intrigues and wars followed between Hyderabad, Delhi and Oudh. The successor to the throne was blinded and a puppet king put in office, only to be murdered. A usurper from Kabul invaded India and attacked the Marathas, who dreamed of restoring a Hindu empire; their dream was shattered, but their power increased steadily. Supported by the British, a blinded king exercised nominal sovereignty. In a struggle with the British for hegemony over the Indian subcontinent the Marathas were defeated. The last Mughul emperor was put on trial by the British and exiled to Rangoon.

When Queen Victoria was proclaimed empress of India on January 1, 1877, the rule of the Islamic sultans and emperors came to an end.

Plates

Quwwat-ul-Islam mosque, Old Delhi

17 The Qutb, viewed from the south. In the foreground: the 'Alai Darwaza gateway.

18 On the Qutb, inscriptions and ornamental bands form a striking contrast to the bold blocks of masonry. The minaret, dedicated to victory, rises directly, without a plinth, from the pavement of the court.

19 Projecting galleries from which the 'mu'azzin' summons the faithful to prayer are supported by corbelled niches, known as stalactites.

20 A narrow spiral staircase in the Qutb is lit from narrow windows not visible from outside. Here, a view into the deep reveal of one of these windows. The Hindu artisans commissioned by the sultan with this work spanned these openings by corbel-vaulting, a construction with which they were familiar.

Fathepur Sikri

21 Fathepur Sikri was the residence of the Great Mughul Akbar. From the Panch Mahal, a five-storeyed pillared structure, we look south-west upon the Jodh Bai palace. In the background: the Buland Darwaza, a triumphal gateway which Akbar had incorporated into the south wing of the mosque to commemorate his invasion of Khandesh.

22 The emperor's living and sleeping apartments are situated along the side of a square lake.

23 The Panch Mahal presumably served as part of the zenana. From here the princesses could look out over the 'pachisi' court.

24–25 In the Diwan-i-Khas, the Public Audience Hall, the emperor would sit upon a throne raised upon a single pillar in the centre.

26 View of the storage rooms in the mint.

27 In the southern part of the palace precinct are stables for horses and camels.

28 General view of the so-called House of Raja Birbal.

29 The House of Raja Birbal is built of red sandstone in close imitation of a timber-framed structure.

30 In the House of Raja Birbal nearly every square inch is covered with finely-textured Islamic ornaments. View from the reveal of a doorway.

31 Consoles on the exterior wall of the House of Raja Birbal. Hindu artists thought mainly in spatial terms, whereas Islamic ones thought two-dimensionally. In the early Mughul style these two traditions are blended, resulting in tension between the massive forms and the fine plastic treatment.

32 The Jami'Masjid at Fathepur Sikri, viewed from one of the side chapels.

33 The dome over this side chapel follows, in form and method of construction, prototypes in wood.

34 In the court of the mosque stands the tomb of the saintly Salim Chishti. This small structure is built wholly of white marble. View of the gallery around it.

35 Monolithic window-screen carved from thin pieces of marble.

36 Detail of one window-screen.

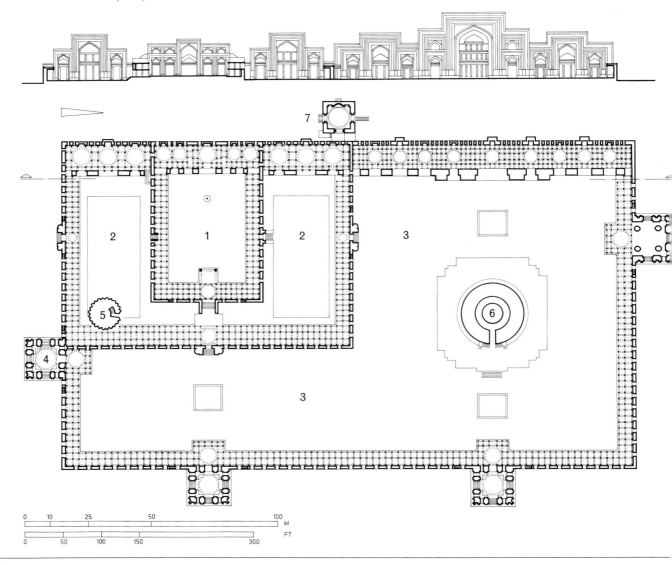

Quwwat-ul-Islam mosque, from 1200
Section and ground-plan 1:1500

1 Original symmetrical plan (1200)
2 First enlargement (1210–1229)
3 Second enlargement (1295–1315)
4 'Alai Darwaza (1305)

5 Qutb Minar (after 1200)
6 Unfinished minaret (after 1310)
7 Iltutmish's tomb (1236)

M

FT

14

Sultan Iltutmish's tomb, built 1236
Section, view and ground-plan 1:250

1 Stalactites, which support the balconies of the Qutb
  Minar

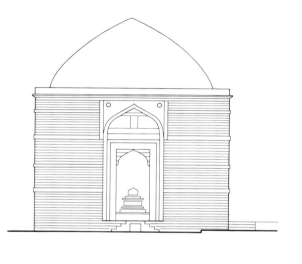

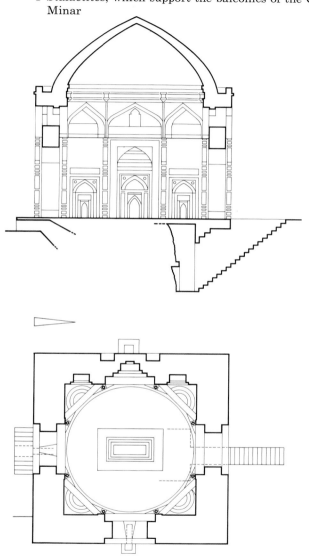

1

Notes

The Qutb Minar in the Quwwat-ul-Islam mosque,
ca. 1200 A.D.

The Qutb Minar is one of those architectural masterpieces whose form owes little to sheer necessity. It is true that a staircase inside leads to circular galleries whence the mu'azzin summons the faithful to prayer; but in this case, if he were to climb to the uppermost galleries, his voice would remain unheard, since the minaret is far higher than this liturgical custom would require.

The idea of erecting a minaret to commemorate a deceased person or a victory was not new, and even the form had precedents, as has been noted in Chapter I. But this does not explain why, in the most varied types of society, men have repeatedly resorted to the column or tower. The reason lies in its symbolic value.

In Hindu architecture the tower and column can have two different meanings, which are not necessarily mutually exclusive. They are either phallic symbols derived from pre-Aryan fertility cults or representations of the cosmic centre or cosmic axis, an idea fundamental to Aryan cosmology.

Also for Qutb-ud-din, the first Muslim sultan of Delhi and the builder of the Qutb Minar, the tower symbolized the axis of the world – especially of the Islamic world which he sought to rule from Delhi.

The word 'rule' gives us the key. Towers, obelisks and monumental columns were erected exclusively by rulers, whether they were sultans, emperors or popes. They are an expression of power, or, to use different terms, the final manifestation in visual form of a sociological change which originated in the Neolithic. We have in mind the transition from the village to the city – the 'urban implosion', as Lewis Mumford put it, that was caused by growing class stratification and the division of labour.

The birth of the city was the first step which enabled man to break out of his narrow concern with the problems of sustaining himself and propagating his species, and to begin to relate his existence to the wider universe. It marked the birth of abstract thought. This period of crystal-lization – as one may call the age that witnessed the foundation of the first cities and the delegation of power to worldly and spiritual leaders – was followed thousands of years later by another, when the very concept of city and ruler became abstracted and crystallized. In this 'second urban implosion' a tower was erected in the centre of the city.

From this it follows that a city or urban district can have only a single tower. It is therefore not surprising that Qutb-ud-din built but a single minaret for his new mosque. In view of its symbolic meaning (see the inscriptions quoted on p. 42) a second minaret would have cancelled out the orderly frame created by the first.

In the plan of the Quwwat-ul-Islam mosque (plan p. 13) a second minaret can indeed be identified. It was begun by one of Qutb-ud-din's successors, Sultan 'Ala-ud-din, but was never finished. Its dimensions show that its erection was not based upon considerations of an architectonic or symbolic character, but was merely the product of this ruler's inordinate ambition and exaggerated self-esteem. Assuming that the proportion between its height and diameter was to have been the same as in the Qutb Minar, it would have measured almost 200 metres in height had it been built.

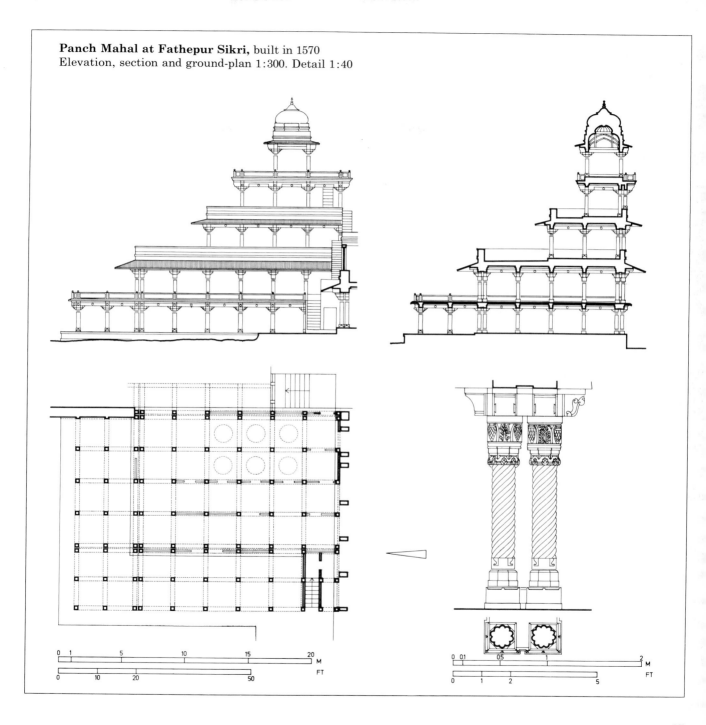

Panch Mahal at Fathepur Sikri, built in 1570
Elevation, section and ground-plan 1:300. Detail 1:40

0 1   5   10   15   20
                                                    M
                                                    FT
0   10   20   50

0 0.1   0.5   1   2
                                                    M
                                                    FT
0   1   2   5

37

Diwan-i-Khas at Fathepur Sikri, built in 1570
Section, elevation and ground-plan 1:250

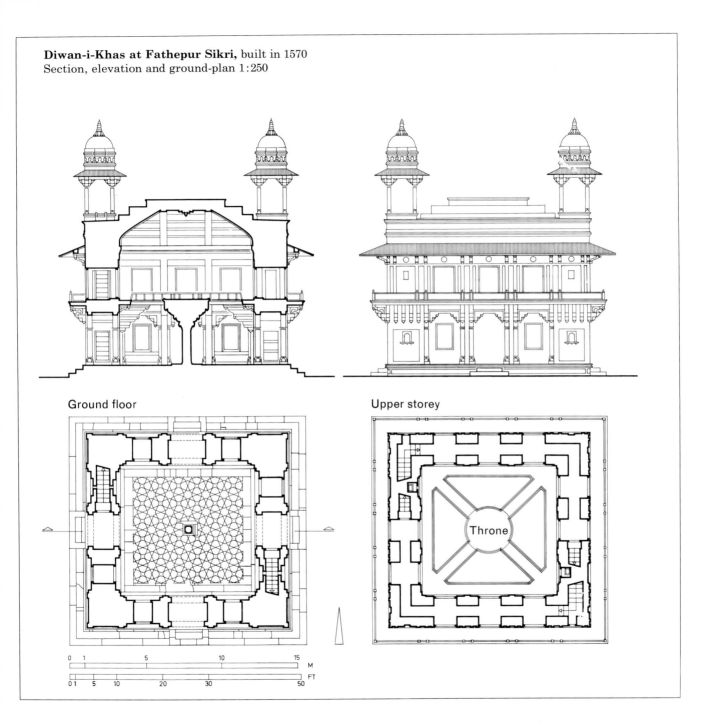

Ground floor

Upper storey

Throne

0 1	5	10	15	
				M

| 0 1 | 5 | 10 | 20 | 30 | 50 | FT |

2. Mosques and Tombs

As soon as the first Muslims settled in India and founded the sultanate of Delhi, they began to build forts, mosques and towers of victory. Since they had no fixed ideas as to the appearance of these buildings, they merely laid down the function they had to fulfil and left their execution to native Hindu craftsmen.

For the invaders it was a divine command to fight a holy war for Islam and to conquer infidels. Even before the Muslims set out to build prayer-halls designed to meet their particular needs they set about razing to the ground Hindu places of worship, invariably referred to by Muslims as Boudh-khana ('Buddha house'). In doing so they developed a special demolition technique that was relatively cheap –the use of elephants. Their hatred and scorn were directed not against particular architectural forms but against the temple as a centre of idolatry. Thus it is not surprising that Qutb-ud-din Aibak, when he decided to construct a huge mosque at Delhi, considered that the spoils of demolished Hindu and Jain temples would prove fitting building material. In addition there could be no more vivid testimony to the Muslims' victory over the pagans than the use of parts of Hindu temples in the prayer-halls of 'the true faith'. Contemporary records state that at Delhi, on the site of a Hindu temple which had been razed to the ground, the conquerors built within three days colonnades to screen off the court of the Qutb mosque from its environs, for which purpose they used the columns of twenty-seven heathen places of worship. Since a mosque was then regarded as no more than an assembly hall–in imitation of the caravanserai, a community building widely disseminated and purposefully planned–the Muslims, in contrast to Hindu temple architects, were not bound by any rules or traditions of the symbolic significance of their work, either in regard to its general layout or in regard to matters of detail. Only one point was laid down in the Koran: anthropomorphic renderings of God and human images were prohibited. Thus from the great number of Hindu sanctuaries earmarked for demolition they chose only those columns, entablatures and similar members, which bore no such figures or ornaments. If an architectural element featured even a small head of a deity, or the representation of a celestial guardian, the offending sculpture was simply hacked off.

It is by no means surprising that it was left to the native sthapatis (Hindu priest-architects) to carry out the designs roughly sketched by the sultan, and that no craftsmen were summoned from Ghazni. For his part Mahmud of Ghazni had built his residence in Afghanistan, one of the most splendid towns in the Orient, with the aid of Indian artisans whom he had captured during his raids into that country. Their fame had thus spread far beyond the frontiers of the Hindukush during the first seven centuries of our era. Hindus worked in Persia as well as in Indo-China. Indian influence upon architecture in the Near East can be seen in numerous details, such as the Buddhist symbol of the solar disk (or Great Wheel) and the triratna (three jewels, trident) on a mosque at Baghdad, or the ornamental Indian form of the 'kumbha' (pot of water) found on other Persian mosques.

Mahmud of Ghazni, in a letter to one of his governors, praised 'the stability and splendour' of the other buildings at Mathura after his conquest of this city. He declared that such impressive cities could only have been constructed at the cost of millions of dinar and in not less than two centuries.

Al-Biruni, a Persian scholar in Mahmud's suite, wrote to his colleagues at the university of Ghazni about the large artificial ponds used by Hindus for bathing:
'In this they have attained an extremely high degree of artistry, so much so that our people, if they were to see these constructions, would be amazed and would be incapable of describing them, let alone building anything similar.'
In view of Al-Biruni's otherwise unflattering remarks, this appraisal of Hindu architecture carries particular conviction.

Thus Qutb-ud-din Aibak found in his empire the most experienced craftsmen's guilds in Asia. He

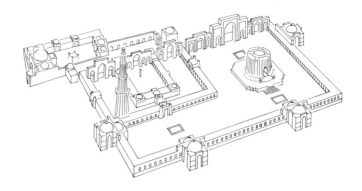

Reconstruction of the Qutb (Quwwat-ul-Islam) mosque in Old Delhi, begun by Sultan Qutb-ud-din Aibak (1206–1210)

commissioned these artisans, who not long before had brought Hindu architecture to a peak of perfection, to dismantle their masterpieces and to reassemble them in the form of a mosque. The outcome of this command, the mosque of Quwwat-ul-Islam ('might of Islam'), also known as the Qutb mosque, actually consisted only of a courtyard enlarged to double its original size, and columns measuring twice their original height, such as one finds in a typical Hindu or Jain temple complex, stripped of its ritual centre, the 'garbha griha' (womb, cella) and the dance halls in front (see grey plan, p. 13/14). The temple court, which in Hindu and Jain architecture was intended to serve as a ritual ambulatory for the sanctuary, became an assembly court for the Muslims, who in their communal prayers faced west.

The orientation of the court toward Mecca led to a more elaborate construction of the western arcade. In the spanning of large areas between the pillars the hand of the Hindu architect was particularly apparent. In imitation of Hindu and Jain halls, cupolas were built as corbelled domes, consisting of rings of stone blocks laid horizontally. The difference in size between a mosque and an Indian temple resulted from the fact that in Hinduism and Jainism the individual expresses his personal worship of God at any time, whereas in Islam the 'mu'azzin' summons the faithful to communal prayer in the mosque (Arabic 'masjid' = 'place of prostration'). Even Qutb-ud-din Aibak, who had few pretensions in matters of aesthetics, saw no satisfactory solution in a mosque hastily put together from spoils. He noted the absence of the familiar pointed arch, the only geometric symbol woven into the prayer rug of faithful Muslims. For centuries the pointed arch, i.e. the ogee arch, had been used by Persian architects to mark off the court of the mosque from the hall on the western side ('liwan').

Three years after the original complex had been finished the sultan ordained that a high wall with apertures in the form of pointed arches should be erected before the liwan. He sketched for the architects what he had in mind by a pointed arch, but evidently was unable to tell them how such an arch was constructed in lands to the west of India which had experienced the influence of Roman architecture. The builders thus had to fall back upon the kind of arch with corbelled courses that was already familiar to them. Only in the uppermost corners, at the point where the two curvatures of the arch met, did this construction prove unsuccessful; here the horizontal joints were turned downwards until finally they were vertical to the curvature of the arch, enabling the arch to be completed. No other monument anywhere

in the world illustrates more clearly the empirical way in which such a basic architectural form as the radiating arch was achieved – a form necessitated by the limited size of the stone modules used.

Hitherto no Indian architect had ever erected a façade, i.e. a wall that was most emphatically vertical. The sultan did not think it unusual to demand an embellishment of this kind for his building. Had it not been the custom for centuries in Muslim camps, everywhere from the Nile to the Indus, to erect, in lieu of a mosque, a skeleton structure from which hung rugs and decorated awnings and which faced towards Mecca? Why should such a provisional arrangement not be translated into the durable form of a building?

Ideas of this kind were quite alien to the sthapati. For him a religious edifice could be nothing other than a divine manifestation, something that he visualized plastically in the same way as the incomprehensible hierarchy of Hindu deities. Without any real understanding for the symbolic value that the arch had for Muslims, the Hindu craftsman resignedly erected a smooth high screen-wall, not so much an architectural member as a curtain-wall. It was only in the detailed work that fruitful collaboration became possible between Hindu artisans and the masters of artistic calligraphy of the Muslim world. Without the aid of Indians who for centuries had been versed in working stone it would have been impossible to resolve the wall into a delicate network of Arabic characters, scrolls and ornamental bands. Even if the sultan had brought Persian craftsmen to Delhi, they would not have been able to cope with the stonemasons' tasks, since in their native land brick and not stone was used in building.

The jubilation of the troops gathered to watch Qutb-ud-din march into Delhi was described by a contemporary in the following words:
'Delhi is the capital of the kingdom and the centre of divine victory and divine aid, honoured and embellished by his royal majesty. The city and the land were filled with joy. It was adorned like the gardens in

Development from corbelled to 'true' arch

a) ancient Indian way of constructing corbelled arch
b) corbelled arch with courses turned down vertically at the crown
c) Indo-Islamic radially cut arch

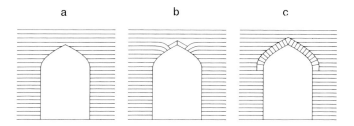

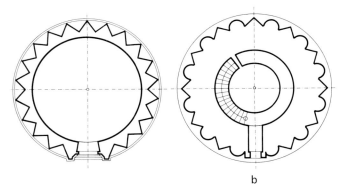

b

Comparison of ground-plan of a Persian and an Indian monumental tower

a) Tomb tower at Rhages
b) Qutb Minar at Old Delhi

Iran; ramparts and gates shone in golden cloths from China and the finest brocades from Constantinople. Here triumphal arches were erected, a splendour to the eye, and so tall that a bird with even the strongest wings could have flown no higher. Observers shuddered as they saw the swords and weapons suspended all about, sparkling in the light. The sultan embellished the great mosque with gold and stones from temples which he caused to be destroyed by elephants, and covered the walls with Tughra inscriptions of the divine commandments.'

Simultaneously with the addition to the mosque of the screen-wall work began on building the tall tower of victory, the Qutb Minar, beside the Quwwat-ul-Islam. In 1199 Qutb-ud-din laid the foundation-stone for this so-called 'Qutb' (axis). Only a tower higher than any that had hitherto been erected seemed to the sultan the appropriate way to demonstrate the victory of Islam over the 'idolaters'. Inscriptions indicate the symbolic significance attributed to this tower. It was built, we are told, to cast God's shadow west and east. Some regarded it as presumptuous to speak of an axis of faith several thousands of miles away from the real centre of Islam, the Ka'ba in Mecca. Others, on the contrary, regarded the Qutb as a sign of the

power of Islam, which was destined to conquer the whole of India.

The tower is 72.5 metres high and tapers towards the top, its diameter decreasing from 15 to about 3 metres. It is the highest edifice in India. The three lower storeys belong to the original design, and formerly terminated in a roof kiosk. The two upper storeys, which differ in treatment and material from the lower ones, were added by Firuz Shah in 1368 after the kiosk had been struck by lightning.

Sepulchral towers with fluting are well known from Persia. That at Rhages, with twenty-two stars in its ground-plan, has an identical diameter to that of the Qutb, and may be regarded as its immediate model, especially as it also anticipates the transition from the star to the projecting circular gallery by means of a cluster of corbelled recesses known as stalactites. It is still difficult to explain why on one hand Persian funerary towers were so familiar at Qutb-ud-din's court yet on the other hand there seems to have been no recollection as to how arches and vaults had been constructed in the same area for almost 1,000 years.

Sultan Iltutmish enlarged the mosque to almost three times its original size by building new colonnades around the old structure, thus also incorporating the minaret whence the 'mu'azzin' summoned the faithful to prayer. To the first arched screen-wall he added two further walls, so that the symmetry of the plan was not disturbed.

At the turn of the thirteenth and fourteenth centuries Ala-ud-din further extended this façade, built a much enlarged courtyard by a second extension, and began to erect a second minaret which, had it ever risen above the first storey, would have overshadowed every tower in the world. This gigantic plan, comparable only to the Egyptian pyramids, was thwarted by the fact that Ala-ud-din, like so many others of his dynasty, fell victim to a conspiracy.

The spatial conception of a mosque was based upon

that of Muhammad's house in Medina. The Prophet had as a matter of principle invited his followers to pray in his own private home, and had rejected every form of sanctuary. Just as he had forbidden the representation of divine beings, so he thought it improper to attribute to any room here on earth some kind of transcendental significance. In this, however, he did not reckon with his followers' love of decoration. For several centuries, it is true, they did allow themselves to be prevented from making figures, but not long after the Prophet's death they began to construct religious buildings. Since 'tradition' formed part of the principles of the faith, as well as the Koran and its interpretations, architects of these monuments kept to the scheme of the ground-plan of Muhammad's house. The latter consisted of a rectangular court surrounded by brick walls, inside which were ranged the living and domestic quarters. Along one side the court was enclosed by a deep hall, of which the flat clay roof was supported by the trunks of palm-trees.

In the sultanate of Gulbarga, one of the southern provinces of the Turkish kingdoms destroyed by Timur, an ingenious fourteenth-century architect had had the idea of reversing all the architectural principles governing mosques with a courtyard. The result was a spatial arrangement resembling that of the mosque at Cordoba. It started from the notion that it was not very sensible to let the faithful kneel in a courtyard without providing them with any protection against the blazing sun in this degree of latitude, while the shady colonnades round about served no proper purpose. Thus in the mosque of Gulbarga the conventional design of the courtyard was filled with small cupolas supported by arches placed close together. In this way, however, the complex lost the precise definition of a courtyard with colonnades round the outer wall. Roofing over the courtyard also brought about a different result. Hitherto it had not been necessary to come to grips with problems of lighting, but now the question arose as to how it was possible to light the interior. Ample lighting through windows was ruled out, since it seemed risky to try to cut windows of sufficient dimensions into the cupolas. Only one possibility therefore

remained: those screen-walls which had been placed in front of the less important arcades on a reduced scale in the western, eastern and southern parts of the court had to be transferred to the hitherto continuous outside walls. Light was now admitted through the circular hall supported on columns (as well as through very small windows in the cupolas of the court). In this way the simple court was turned into a multi-partite structure, of which only one corresponding example exists in India: the 'mandapas' of contemporary Jain and Hindu temples (see p. 151).

The problems facing architects in translating into reality such a wholly new spatial concept led them to ask some basic questions about the use of pointed arches, barrel-vaulting and domes. The upshot was a structure of academic simplicity in which all the restrictive fetters of Hindu and Islamic tradition were shaken off. A type of building evolved in which the arch underwent an extraordinary range of variations (see grey plan p. 171). It has three characteristics.

(1) Use was made only of arches and domes.

(2) The span of the arches varied, in order to distinguish between the court area and the former colonnade.

As a result of the second characteristic, (a) the forest of supporting columns in the court was clearly delimited by expansion of the circular zone (if this were not the case, the forest of supporting columns would dissolve); (b) the façades were thereby accentuated at the corners, at the point of the columnar interval – as is unavoidable with an elongated building (cf. in this connection the contraction of the final columnar interval in Greek colonnades, or the bossage work in the denticules of Renaissance palaces).

The supports arranged in a square in the court and the extended axis of the circular zone make it impossible for both the court and the hall to be roofed over in the same way. Above the square panels domes are erected, whereas over the rectangular ones we find barrel-vaulting which in cross-section repeats the form of the arches. In the corners of the building large square areas are formed, i.e. larger domes.

(3) The third characteristic of the arch is that the small cupolas of the court span one section of the plan, while the larger ones at the corners span four sections. The space in front of the mihrab on the west side is integrated by a large dome covering nine sections. This dome gives the entire complex a fixed point and determines its orientation.

As a result of this third feature we may note the following: since the large dome is the optic centre, seen both from within and from outside, it has to be elevated above the general level of the building, i.e. be placed upon a square platform or drum.

The mosque at Gulbarga in India is not based upon any known prototype. The Bahmani dynasty, which was based upon Gulbarga, was founded by the servant of a Brahmin at the court of Muhammad Tughluq. However, this connection with the court of Delhi is not evident from the style of these buildings. The fort in the walls of which the mosque stands is decorated predominantly with spoils from Hindu temples.

The plans for this mosque can only have been devised by a lone individual architect or by the king himself. Unfortunately this exemplary design did not catch on, perhaps because of the mullahs, who saw maintenance of tradition as one of their duties. But it is equally possible that news of the new type of building could not penetrate across the borders of antagonistic sultanates. When the Bahmani kingdom was absorbed into the Mughul empire in 1609, Gulbarga had already for two centuries been a deserted and ruined provincial town, incapable of providing any stimulus for the best Mughul architects.

The mosque at Gulbarga owes its charm above all to a number of experiments in the use of space that are unconventional in Indian architecture, which led to its austerity of composition: as the rooms are approximately the same height, the spanning of the large areas between the supports in the circular zone

reduced the height of the arches and so made the shafts unusually short. The height of the arch to its apex is equal to its breadth, in other words the arch and the shaft may be inscribed within a square (see p. 152).

The broad spacing between the outer arches makes for tension between them and the arches of the court, which for this reason look slender. A further enhancement is obtained when one views the monument along the diagonals of the ground-plan, where the intersecting arches resemble a fluting of closely packed stilts.

In many provinces or independent sultanates masterpieces were constructed in the fourteenth and fifteenth centuries which can only be mentioned briefly here.

Jaunpur, near Benares, was originally the capital

Jami'Masjid at Jaunpur, built in 1470

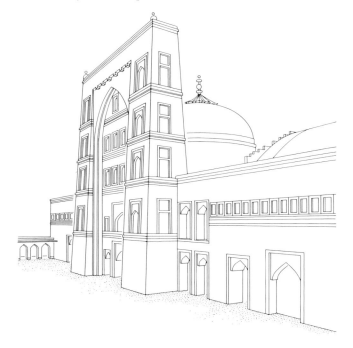

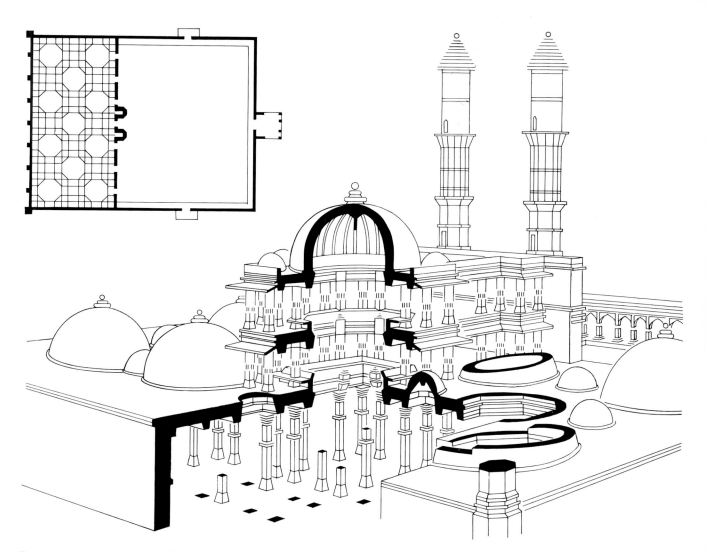

Ground-plan and cut-away diagram of the Jami'Masjid at Champanir, built in 1485

of the eastern Tughluq lands, and then, when the empire began to disintegrate after Timur's invasion, became the seat of the Sharqi dynasty. The Jami' Masjid at Jaunpur can without doubt be derived stylistically from the Tughluq monuments at Delhi, the most characteristic of which, Tughluq's mausoleum, we shall discuss in connection with other tombs. All later mosques at Jaunpur, which are laid out on the plan of the Jami'Masjid, are distinguished by having particularly lofty 'liwan' portals, whose sloping walls recall Egyptian pylons. It is the gateway that is brought into focus, whereas the dome behind is not visible to the eye. This solution seems justified, since only the dominating wall of the portal can replace the orienting function of the mihrab, which as a rule is not visible to the thousands of faithful assembled in the courtyard. It did not seem appropriate to draw their attention to a huge dome behind the low portal, since a static form such as the dome lacks the orienting capacity found in the arch.

An entirely different course of development occurred in Gujarat province, in whose temporary capital, Champanir, the final phase of evolution is marked by a peculiar mosque. Its ground-plan seems to be of classical simplicity: a rectangle with sides in the proportion 4:5 is divided longitudinally in the proportion 2:3 (2 for the liwans, 3 for the court); the broad pillared hall of the liwan terminates in eleven staggered domes, an arrangement of Persian origin. Since the domes were all the same height, one would expect them to be similar in elevation. But the elevation shows that it was decided–possibly not until the building was actually being erected–to introduce a new motif in the vertical development, which could not be inferred from the ground-plan, namely, to give the nave three storeys.

It may possibly be a sign of decadence for the ground-plan and the elevation of a monument to bear so little relation to one another as they do in Champanir. The optical impression is not felicitous, for it looks as though a Jain temple has been grafted on to a mosque. Thus collaboration between Hindus and Muslims was not always successful. The halls with supporting columns and the various kinds of dome are typically Hindu or Jain, whereas the ground-plan is austerely Islamic in conception, such as we find in Persia and Asia Minor.

Let us follow this development in the chief centres of Indo-Islamic architecture, Agra, Delhi and Fathepur Sikri. The palaces at Fathepur Sikri are situated in the centre of the city on a ridge, with the mosque standing on the very summit. It is the largest monument in the city and determines the traditional orientation of the surrounding palaces towards the four cardinal points. Like all imperial monuments, it is built in red sandstone which is quarried on the spot. The palaces, caravanserai, administrative buildings and stables show the Great Mughul Akbar's liking for simple Hindu methods of building, whereas the

mosque constitutes an exception with its frequent use of pointed arches and domes.

Let us now consider the reconstruction of this mosque in its original state. It is surprising to find several changes in the ground-plan by comparison with the traditional layout of the court, which as a rule was modelled upon Muhammad's house. These changes can only be attributed to strong influence by a Hindu architect. This is genuine 'Hinduization', which affects the general plan and not merely certain details. Hitherto the courtyard, roofed on the west side, formed a unit. In the mosque at Fathepur Sikri, as a consequence of Akbar's tolerant attitude, Hindu architects had the opportunity to realize their own idea of the way in which a court should be related to a sanctuary. As in their own temples they designed a court enclosed on all four sides by identical arcades.

Jami'Masjid at Fathepur Sikri, built in 1571

a) reconstruction of original state
b) enlargement during reign of Akbar

1. Salim Chishti's tomb
2. royal gate
3. Buland Darwaza, victory gate
4. Islam Khan's tomb

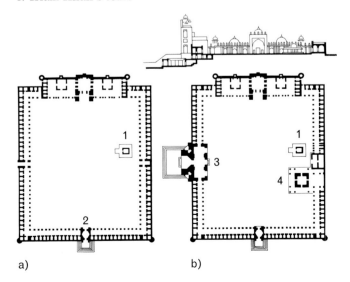

a)   b)

The sanctuary, which in a Hindu temple always stood in the centre, naturally now had to be moved to the west side of the court, but was set off against the sanctuary and treated as a detached building. A further step in Hinduization was taken by dividing the liwan hall into a principal sanctuary and two ancillary ones–just as though this were a place for worship of the holy trinity of Vishnu, Shiva and Brahma.

The circular arrangement of the cells (in a traditional mosque there would be no more than an arcade without any adjoining rooms) also featured ancient Indian motifs, taken from Buddhist monasteries and adapted. This is clear from monolithic copies of the rock-cut monasteries at Ajanta. Islamic scholars or mullahs now inhabited rings of cells once occupied by Buddhist monks, or later Hindu or Jain temples containing idols. Thus the mosque at Fathepur Sikri was not only the assembly-place of the faithful, but also the municipal university and monastery, just as had been the case in Buddhist and Hindu cultural centres. Several years after the Jami'Masjid had been completed, the emperor caused its symmetrical plan to be modified by the addition and reconstruction of various parts. The tomb of the saintly Salim Chishti may have been originally planned to stand inside the courtyard. But the white marble structure stems from as late as Jahangir's reign. All the other buildings, such as the tomb of Islam Khan, a grandson of Salim Chishti, are placed asymmetrically and are definitely not part of the original plan.

Twenty-five years after the mosque had been completed, when Akbar returned to Fathepur Sikri from a triumphant campaign into the Deccan, he decided to erect a victory arch. It seems incomprehensible to us that he should have chosen to site it at the south gate of the mosque, of all places; for when entering the mosque from the direction of his palaces, through the east gate, he would see only its plain rear side. Presumably he was particularly insistent that the Buland Darwaza ('lofty portal') should be visible from afar, and this could be achieved only by building it on the south side.

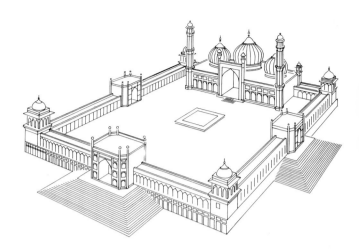

Jami'Masjid at Delhi, the largest mosque in India, built between 1644 and 1658 by the Great Mughul Shah Jahan

Let us now compare the Jami'Masjid of Shah Jahan at Delhi–the last great mosque to be built during the Mughul period–with that at Fathepur Sikri. The attempt at Fathepur Sikri to develop a specifically Indo-Islamic form of mosque by incorporating native ideas was taken over by Shah Jahan's architects and culminated in the altogether classical form of the mosque at Delhi. It cannot be excluded that, on being commissioned to build this mosque, the largest in India, the architects first studied the mosque at Fathepur Sikri. They adhered to this prototype in so far as it met their strict standards, and only altered the plan in regard to certain weaknesses. In this way the plan of the Delhi mosque acquired a unique degree of clarity. If the mosque at Gulbarga represents, as we have seen, a classical solution of the roofed mosque which was hardly capable of further development, in the same way the Jami'Masjid at Delhi emerges as the ultimate stage in the logical evolution of the mosque with a court. The division of the complex into two parts, building and enclosed court, also continued on the west side, is more pronounced at Delhi than at Fathepur Sikri. In the latter case this division was identifiable only from the ground-plan (the cells, arranged in a circle, and the liwan had the same height up to the eaves, and were surmounted by kiosks of the same size), whereas in the mosque at Delhi the building is distinctly set off against the low arcades. Still greater clarity is obtained by not incorporating the façade of the liwan into the ambulatory but by projecting the building so far into the court that the rear wall of the liwan was flush with the wall surrounding the arcade.

At Fathepur Sikri the architects had not made up their minds how to distribute the four round towers in the complex, which from the exterior looked like a fort; at Delhi, on the other hand, kiosks were erected at all four corners of the ambulatory. At Fathepur Sikri the elevated situation of the court resulted in a splendid flight of steps at the entrance. This feature was retained at Delhi, for which purpose an artificial terrace was constructed. The building was thus set off against its environs, as had formerly been the case with Hindu temples.

In building each mosque the architects faced the problem of co-ordinating the dome and the liwan portal. At Fathepur Sikri it had been decided to let the dome—regarded purely as a structural member—disappear completely behind the high wall of the portal. We have encountered the same solution at Jaunpur. It was not ideal, since only a short distance separated the dome and the portal wall, whereas any dome needs some space around it in order to breathe, as it were. The flat corbelled domes of early Indo-Islamic buildings were unpretentious, like the earlier Jain ones. But the higher the dome was made to rise, the more dominant it appeared and the more space it needed for optical reasons.

The most popular type of dome during Shah Jahan's reign was the lotus or bulbous dome. It was almost impossible to incorporate it into a complex of different architectural elements which it had to crown. The lower the portal wall, the more impressive the dome became. Already at an early date these considerations were taken into account at Bijapur, where the architects were careful not to build the façades of the liwan too high. But in Northern India, in conformity with Persian prototypes, monumental repetition of the mihrab was indispensable in the case of an imperial mosque. At Delhi architects found a reasonable compromise by placing the domes of Jami'Masjid on a drum and keeping the distance from the portal wall as great as possible.

Whereabouts in the layout of the Jami'Masjid were the minarets to be located? The symmetry would be destroyed if a single minaret were to be placed next

Plan of the 'Pearl Mosque', built of marble by Aurangzib (1658–1707) in the Red Fort at Delhi

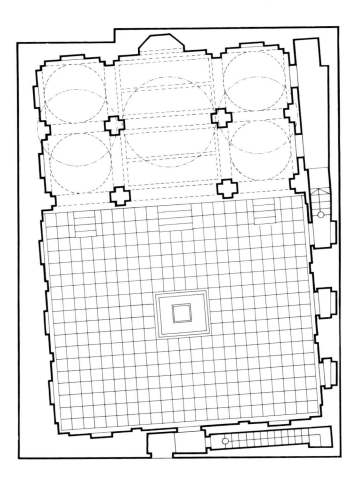

to the mosque, as was the case in Persia or Egypt, or even elsewhere in Delhi, as in the Qutb mosque. Two minarets flanking the portal wall, as at Champanir, would offer too much competition to the main dome. An arrangement whereby four minarets would be erected at the corners of the court was also unsuitable, since they would have to be oriented towards a central point, as in the Taj Mahal. Moreover, efforts were actually being made to concentrate all the spatial emphases upon a single point in order to turn the liwan hall into a Hindu-style sanctuary. The one remaining possibility was to place two minarets at the corners of the liwan which jutted far into the court. In this way they would not overshadow the lotus-shaped domes, yet would still lend emphasis to the sanctuary.

While the Mughul emperors looked more and more towards Persian monumental buildings, until they finally omitted all Hindu elements from their edifices, in its spatial articulation the mosque gradually came to approximate more closely to the Hindu temple.

During the reign of Aurangzib building slackened, and progress in other branches of art diminished. Every day, as he proceeded from the Red Fort to Jami'Masjid, the bigoted emperor saw himself surrounded by an ill-disposed population. Since it was embarrassing for him to have to cross the town, he had a small mosque built for himself in the precincts of his palace. His ancestors had vied with one another by building ever larger public mosques. Aurangzib sought peace in prayer; the so-called 'Pearl Mosque' (Moti Masjid) was intended solely for his personal use. Since the axes of the Red Fort are not aligned exactly with the cardinal points, but the 'qibla' had to be adhered to precisely, the enclosure wall of this mosque was built with two layers, as it were; the outer layer was adapted to the layout of the palace, while the inner one was twisted in relation to the outer one and followed the orientation exactly.

Sepulchral monuments

As a rule Hindus cremate their dead, scattering the

ashes in a river, if possible into the sacred river Ganges. The Muslims, on the other hand, bury their dead in tombs. The chamber has to be high enough for the deceased to sit upright when he has to account for his worldly conduct to the angels on the first night after his burial. The tomb itself must thus be a spacious structure.

According to the Hindu concept the dead live a formless existence, beyond the limits of space and time, unless they have escaped from the cycle of continuous reincarnation, or have already entered Brahman. It would thus be foolish to build a tomb to contain the ashes of a deceased person. As for the Muslim, after death he must hold out in his tomb until the angel Israfil's trumpet summons him to Judgment Day. The belief in an individual existence after death, bound by limitations of time and space, explains the layout of Islamic tombs, which are always lavishly decorated according to the spiritual and worldly power of the deceased. Just as Muhammad had preached in vain against the building of sanctuaries, so also his ban on the construction of splendid tombs remained ineffective. This may be partly due to the fact that the Prophet's allusion to the merit conferred upon those who visited tombs led to pilgrimages to such monuments, which sooner or later were bound to become lavishly embellished.

Canopy tombs

The construction of a dome above a square of columns was a problem which Hindu and Jain architects had had to face before the Muslim invasion. The usual kind of construction was as follows. Short architraves were laid across the corners, so that the square of the architraves gave the shape of an octagon. Where larger areas had to be spanned, this octagon was given extra support at the eight corners. In this way it was possible to cover relatively spacious dance or sacrificial pavilions. The Jain temple on Mount Abu, for example, illustrates how rings of stones were piled up over the octagon and the size of the aperture was progressively reduced until it could be topped by a capstone.

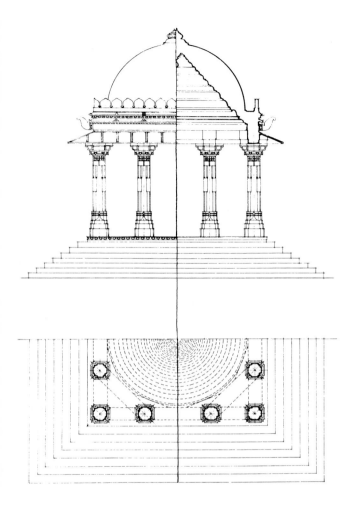

Canopied pavilion constructed in the Hindu manner, with supporting pillars, consoles, 'chayas' and 'false dome'

Indo-Islamic canopy tombs are built in the same manner. This mode of construction gave them the shape of a truncated cone. According to Islamic architectural concepts, however, the dome could not be trapezoid in outline but had to be circular. For this reason the Hindu craftsmen made the exterior of these corbelled domes approximate more closely to a hemispherical shape by applying thick layers of mortar. Apart from this Islamizing feature, these canopy tombs are in all respects of native origin.

Masonry mausolea

The tomb of Persian origin is a compact masonry structure, square or octagonal in ground-plan. The dome is not built up of corbelled courses of stone but consists of voussoirs or bricks set radially.

The first monumental Islamic tomb in India was the mausoleum of Iltutmish, which is part of the Quwwat-ul-Islam mosque in Old Delhi (see grey plan, p. 13/14). From a stylistic point of view it is related to Persian tombs by virtue of its two-dimensional ornaments hewn out of the sandstone. The small square sepulchral chamber has been transformed into an octagon by placing pointed arches diagonally, so producing one of the most common Indo-Islamic intermediate forms in the so-called 'phase of transition': conical vaulting, called squinch. Forerunners can be traced back to Sassanid architecture by way of Mesopotamia; later development in India led to intricate 'draping' in rooms and ceilings.

Like the first sultans, Iltutmish was dependent upon Hindu craftsmen when he had this tomb built shortly before his death in 1235. He laid down the Islamic character of the building in a few guiding principles, of which the most important were probably the treble mihrab arrangement on the west side, the use of the pointed arch and the dome, and the lavish furnishing of the interior by the use of inscribed bands. The clumsy construction of the arches and squinches suggests that Hindu architects were employed. The variety of intertwined ornaments and the way in which all the interior areas are resolved into a fine stone texture illustrate the readiness of the first Islamic sovereigns to let the natives give full rein to their imagination.

A puritanical reaction set in during the reign of Ghiyas-ud-din Tughluq I, one of Ala-ud-din's generals, who as a result of his victories in battle against successive Mongol invaders had risen to the rank of viceroy of the Punjab and finally usurped the throne of Delhi. Tughluq, who was not so much an aristocrat as a military commander, had little love for the luxury with which the sultan had surrounded himself at Delhi, and spent his time on horseback defending the empire against the Mongol hordes.

Tughluq I's son and successor – and murderer – built a splendid fortress-tomb at Tughluqabad, the residence of the Tughluq dynasty near Old Delhi. This tomb is a small fort, irregular in ground-plan, situated in the middle of an artificial lake. By means of a bridge carried on arches this complex was linked to the wall of his fort at Tughluqabad, giving the impression of a small projecting bastion. The tomb was constructed in every detail as a veritable stronghold. As in all Oriental fortresses, the entrance is staggered and the enclosure walls have apertures for embrasures. The peculiar feature of this mausoleum is that even the walls of the square tomb are sloping.

It is not possible here to trace all the kinds of tomb that evolved up to the Mughul period. In rough outline the course of development was as follows. Cubic buildings whose prototype in India was the tomb of Iltutmish, became larger, acquired two-storeyed façades, and increasingly lost the slope of their outer

Tomb of Ghiyas-ud-din Tughluq I, a small fortress on an artificial lake, built in 1325

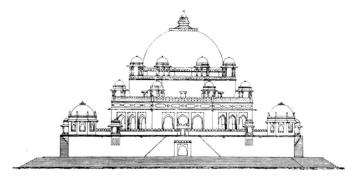

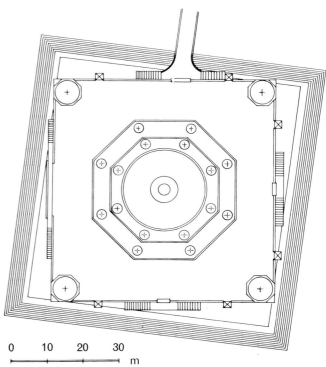

0   10   20   30
├────┼────┼────┤
                m

Sher Shah's tomb at Saseram, a stately pavilion built on an island in an artificial lake (1540); vertical section of the tomb

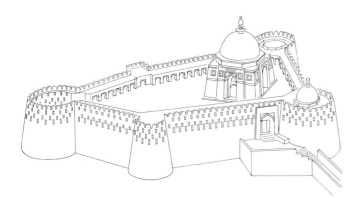

walls. To articulate the bare walls a projection in the centre was accentuated by adding a high rectangular portal with a pointed arch. The areas on both

51

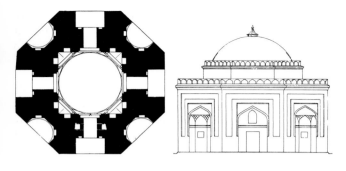

Tomb no. 36 at Delhi, with its square interior and octagonal exterior, differs in shape from the others

sides of the porch were provided with four niches. In imitation of the 'panch-ratna' type of Hindu temple, the spandrels of the flat roof were crowned by four small kiosks. If we study the diagonals of the ground-plan, we find that they form a pleasing transition from the circular dome to the cube of the walls.

Octagonal buildings were occasionally surrounded by an arcade whose roofs, like the spandrels of the square roofs, were crowned by kiosks modelled on canopy tombs. In the environs of Delhi we find a particularly large number of octagonal tombs. The most recent and fully developed monumental form is represented by a mausoleum at Bihar which was built for Sher Shah, the opponent of Humayun, at Saseram during the Mughul period. Like Tughluq's tomb, that of Sher Shah is situated in an artificial lake. This tomb is, however, not conceived as a defensive structure of masonry, but as a differentiated composition of courtly kiosks. It is no longer separated from the water by the wall of a fort but has access to the water on all sides by flights of steps. Tughluq's tomb was a functional structure screened off from the outside world; the tomb of Sher Shah displays its features as a memorial toward all points of the compass, clearly manifesting its Hindu symbolism.

Of particular interest in the discussion of Mughul tombs that follows are several small octagonal tombs with square interiors. A building of this kind may be regarded either as primarily square with sloping corners or as octagonal with niches in the interior making it look square. The ingenious fusion of forms –and the confusion which results from any analysis of them–was no doubt the work of Hindu architects who for centuries had dallied with the circle and square–the basic symbols of Hindu metageometry– in the temple-towers of Northern India. The blend of octagonal and square ground-plans led them to specific Indo-Islamic solutions to the spatial problems presented by the mausoleum.

Mughul tombs

Although Babur, the first Mughul, gave strong encouragement to all the arts, the chaos of war left him little time in which to execute bold architectural projects. In his memoirs he mentions various gardens and monuments, but since these were functional buildings his successors did not bother to preserve them. Concerning one of the mosques he built he wrote: 'It is not beautiful; it is built in the Hindustani style'. This remark alone goes to show that his dynasty was not disposed to allow Hindu architects to carry out their plans indiscriminately. Henceforward each ruler exerted an active influence upon individual designs and thus coined a personal style restricted to his own reign, which gave way to the equally personal style of his successor.

The development of Mughul architecture is closely linked with the fate that befell the second Mughul. Humayun, who had lived at the court of Shah Tahmasp, brought to Delhi from his place of exile not only a large Persian army but also no doubt a galaxy of Persian courtiers, artists and architects. When the sovereign died shortly after the Mughul empire had been restored, he was buried on the bank of the Jumna. His widow, Haji Begum, settled here together with her Persian court, founded a small colony, and dedicated herself wholly to the task of building for her late consort a unique mausoleum. She had lived in Persia with Humayun and now commissioned a

Persian by the name of Mirak Mirza Ghiyas with the planning and execution of this project (see grey plan, p. 78). He was assisted by architects and craftsmen, the majority of whom were likewise foreigners. This is evident both from the Persian style of the tomb and from the name 'Arab Serail' borne by the artisans' dwellings outside the precincts, which survive to this day.

If we compare Humayun's tomb with the surrounding octagonal tombs of the Lodi dynasty, we may see what a decisive step had been taken in Indian architecture with the construction of this complex. Hindu elements such as the architrave and corbel were without exception superseded by the pointed arch. Instead of covering the outer surface of the wall with sculptures, it was faced with red sandstone and white marble in imitation of the tiling on Persian tombs, in which large pieces were cut from a sheet and laid as

Geometric analysis of Humayun's tomb at Delhi, built in 1565

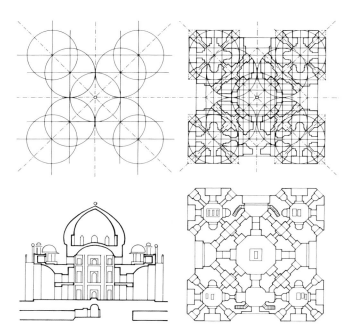

mosaic. The false dome anticipates the exterior of later Mughul buildings; for the first time in India it is here placed over an inner shell of masonry which seals off the interior.

Another innovation, so far as India was concerned, was to place the tomb in a garden. Its strictly geometric articulation followed exactly that of the Persian 'char-bagh' ('four gardens'), which was divided by two axial paths into four squares.

Since the spatial concepts of Persian architects are less comprehensible to us today than one might assume from a brief glance at their work, especially in comparison with Hindu monuments, it is necessary to try to analyse this type of building from several points of view. Today we take exception as a general principle to false constructions such as the double dome. We find it even harder to understand how a refined sense of proportion could have led architects to superpose the inner shell of the dome neither at the base of the circular drum nor on the springing of the outer dome, but instead on an indefinable point halfway between these two altitude markers. Does the double dome serve any purpose at all in this special case? The rounded shape of its inner face of white temper affords no fixed point whereby one can orient oneself or even judge the height of the interior. Why then not lead straight on into the outer dome? Even if the interior had been fashioned in an equally unfathomable manner, the spatial impression would hardly have suffered from excessive elevation. One might go on to ask what could have lent more charm to such a simple interior as this than an addition to the height, to make it correspond to the exterior of the building. These questions can best be answered in geometric terms. The studies by M. Dieulafoy show how greatly Persian monumental architecture is determined by geometric relationships. A very impressive example is his analysis of the tomb of Sultan Muhammad Shah Khudabanda at Sultaniyeh. We may offer a geometric analysis of Humayun's tomb, which, however, must be restricted to the ground-plan since accurate elevations are not yet available (cf. analysis of ground-plan of Taj Mahal, pp. 97–8).

In considering the ground-plan of Humayun's tomb the question arises as to the basic idea that underlies the design. We find here no spatial relationship between the main chamber, the vestibules and the corner spaces. Each space is symmetrical in itself and bears no relationship to any other. This concept also finds expression in the shape of the exterior. The emphatically projecting corner buildings are cut off at their corners and also toward the huge portal. They look like independent buildings, since they are separated from the main part by five façades of their octagonal ground-plan; moreover, their shape is related only to their own symmetrical axes and not to the axes of the main building. This formal independence is further enhanced by the fact that the façades of the corner buildings are absolutely square, i.e. they are self-sufficient entities. In such a conception, we may well ask, where does the main building fit in? One looks for it beneath the dome, but it is precisely here that the deep niches of the portal are carved into the masonry, shifting the centre of gravity of the façades to the corner buildings. Judging by the façades, the main space in the centre can hardly be more than the area remaining between four of the octagonal buildings and the connecting gates. Only the dome links the separate parts of the building and affords the centre the emphasis it lost in favour of the corner buildings.

This design produces tensions that are desirable so long as they do not lead to dissolution of the building in the literal sense of the word. The raised dome – it is much higher than the corner buildings – gives an impression of serenity, with its white marble facing and lack of any of that inlay work which otherwise gives a rhythmic effect to all parts of the building; it is a skilfully chosen means of counteracting the outward pressures and of integrating all the various parts of the building.

If we compare this most Persian of all Indian mausolea with its Persian forerunners, we find that it has been most delicately embellished by extensive use of stone in the building and as facing. Persian monuments were invariably constructed of cheap

materials and are encased in glittering polychrome tiles or bricks, so that they are not uniform in material, construction, form or colour. Things were different in India, where the Mughul emperors had at their disposal an inexhaustible wealth of materials and could afford to put up some massive buildings constructed of materials which had hitherto been used only as casing.

In the account by the British traveller William Finch, who spent some time in Delhi a few decades after the tomb was finished, we read:
'On the left hand is seene the carkasse of old Dely, called the nine castles and fiftie two gates, now inhabited onely by Googers. A little short is a stone bridge of eleven arches, over a branch of Gemini [the Jumna]; from hence a broad way shaded with great trees leading to the sepulchre of Hamaron [Humayun], this kings grandfather, in a large roome spread with rich carpets, the tombe itselfe covered with a pure white sheet, a rich semiane over head, and a front certaine bookes on small tressels, by which stand his sword, tucke [turban] and shooes[5].'

The architects who served the Muslim rulers increasingly moved away from the formal canon of Hindu architecture and developed an individual Indo-Islamic idiom. We may distinguish two phases in this development.

The early Mughul style comprises the monuments built during the reigns of Akbar and Jahangir (approx. 1556–1628). The material used was mostly red sandstone, occasionally with white marble intarsia. Whereas the design of tombs was strongly influenced by the taste of the rulers in question, palaces were still under the sway of traditional Indian forms and structures. The late Mughul style comprises the monuments built during the reigns of Shah Jahan and Aurangzib (approx. 1628–1707). The material used was predominantly white marble. The engrailed arch supersedes the simple pointed arch. The contours of the monuments testify to a refined effeminate taste.

The extent to which architecture was influenced

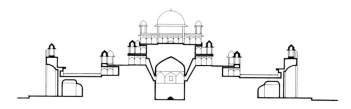

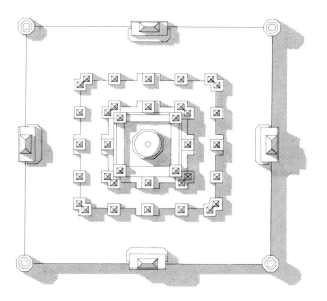

The mausoleum of the Great Mughul Akbar was built as a tiered pyramid, following the model of ancient Indian monasteries

by the ruler's taste is shown in the two mausolea of Akbar and Jahangir. Akbar began to design and build his tomb while he was still alive. It marks a departure from Persian tradition and the adoption of elements drawn predominantly from Buddhist and Hindu traditions. A tiered pyramid, inspired by Buddhist monasteries of wood, culminates in an open terrace upon which stands a copy of the marble coffin. The sarcophagus itself is located in the centre of the massive pyramid. The 'mountain and cave' motif was no doubt borrowed from the Hindu symbolic idiom.

The tomb which Jahangir designed for himself at Shahdara near Lahore was completed only after the death of his consort, Nur Jahan. It is a very conventional one-storeyed flat building, situated in the middle of a large park on the bank of a river, like most Mughul tombs (see p. 85).

The transition from the early to the late Mughul style is best illustrated by a building which belongs to Jahangir's reign but was not planned by him. This is the tomb built by Nur Mahal, Jahangir's wife, for her father, I'timad-ud-daula, the emperor's Lord High Treasurer and Wazir (see grey plan, p. 129). According to tradition Jahangir, who much preferred miniature painting to architecture, put unlimited resources at his wife's disposal for this project. Only such exceptional circumstances could have produced a work which in costliness is surpassed only by the Taj Mahal. The complex is admittedly not large, since the deceased was not of royal blood. An attempt was made to offset the building's modest scale by covering nearly every square centimetre with the most precious intarsia of marble and precious stones.

This square mausoleum is situated amidst gardens on the east bank of the Jumna, outside the ancient city of Agra. The garden is planned as a char-bagh, modelled on the tombs of Akbar and Humayun. The basic quadripartite division of the garden is overlaid by the mausoleum platform, which together with the path around it is exactly as large as one of the four square segments. According to the accepted scheme, it was surrounded on three sides by high walls, while the fourth fronted on to the river. On the axes are some splendid entrance gates, two of them dummies. Four pavilions mark off the corners.

The ground-plan of this tomb may seem to us lacking in imagination if we bear in mind the ingenious attempts made by architects in the Mughul period to lend each tomb new spatial accents and to find a symbolic idiom with an individual relationship to the deceased. Eight intersecting walls produce nine small rooms, of which five are square; the one in the middle is only a little larger than those in the corners.

This ground-plan is of no symbolic importance, unless one imputes to the architect the intention to express the simple rational intellect of the Lord High Treasurer. Nor has the elevation any surprises in store for us. Flat stucco vaulting spans the low rooms and traditional pavilions enclose the towers at the corners. One cannot reject out of hand the idea that this was not conceived as a tomb but may have been a copy of a dwelling-house that played some part in the treasurer's life. The low ground-floor, devoid of any monumental domed space and possessing only a few windows, is reminiscent of contemporary dwellings, as is the square room surrounded by marble lattice screens on the roof. During this period high airy rooms such as these, in which even a faint breath of wind makes the oppressive heat of the tropical night more bearable, were placed on the flat roofs of many dwelling-houses and palaces.

Floor in kiosk on roof of I'timad-ud-daula's tomb. Two scroll systems run through the inlay work of multi-coloured marble tesserae

The tomb of I'timad-ud-daula is of special interest to us on account of the first use of marble to face all the walls and also of a kind of intarsia known as 'pietra dura'. For the lining Akbar had almost invariably chosen red sandstone and only occasionally caused inlay work to be carried out in marble. It was left to Nur Mahal to choose polychrome precious stones for inlay work and mosaic, with a base of marble. The relationship between dark and light areas is thus reversed. The geometrical motifs of the intarsia, ranged freely in clusters, alternate with fine marble tracery which can only be worked with a file, not a chisel, as was also the case with the filigree work in the Jain marble temples on Mount Abu. Although all these forms are clearly of Persian origin, neither intarsia nor stone tracery could have been realized with such perfection had it not been for the Hindu tradition of stone-working. Among the many details which ought to be mentioned here, let us single out one: the floor of the pavilion on the roof, upon which stands the cenotaph of I'timad-ud-daula and his consort.

The inlay work on this floor shows how much freedom the craftsman had to adapt asymmetrical features to regular scrollwork. He started from the basic form of the scroll and only changed its length, not its course. Our plates depict the basic forms and intertwining of two scroll systems superimposed one on another; they are so densely interwoven that the regularities of the design can no longer be detected.

Plates

Agra (Akharabad)

61 The Red Fort was built by Akbar on the ruins of an ancient fortress.

62 The Jahangiri Mahal, a well-preserved palace, lies within the walls of the Red Fort at Agra. The formal canon of its vast reception hall is borrowed from Hindu architecture.

63 Massive supports mark off the southern reception hall from the court. Persian influence is manifest in the detail, as at Fathepur Sikri.

64 Floral designs and scrollwork cover the supporting pillars. The fine-grained local sandstone also made it possible to render the finest details.

65 The northern reception hall, viewed from the gallery. To bridge the wide span of the ceiling, the emperor's Hindu architects employed struts which perform a function comparable to the struts of a roof truss supported by purlins.

Humayun's tomb near Delhi

66 The mausoleum, situated in a park, viewed from the south.

67 Detail from the lower storey. All parts of the building are faced with red marble; the inlay work is executed in white marble.

68 Humayun, who had lived in exile at the court of the Persian Shah, brought with him to India Persian architects and types of building.

69 Since the tradition of Indian stone-working had been maintained for centuries in Delhi, this 'Persian' mausoleum was not faced with coloured tiles, like its prototypes at Isfahan, but with red sandstone quarried in various parts of Northern India.

70 View into the dome above the sepulchral chamber. The transition from the octagonal zone to the rounded springing of the dome is effected by clusters of squinch nets.

71 Passages connect the galleries between the ancillary rooms in the upper storey of the corner buildings.

I'timad-ud-daula's Mausoleum, Agra

72 The mausoleum, with its white marble facing, viewed from the entrance to the precinct. Seen from any angle, the monument looks rectangular. From the façades it is not apparent that, for example, the kiosk on the roof is absolutely square.

73 Details of the gateway and tomb.

74 The kiosk on the roof viewed diagonally. In the background: the River Jumna.

75 The interior of the kiosk on the roof. In the foreground: replicas of the sarcophagi of I'timad-ud-daula and his consort. The intarsia on the floor and walls is of precious stones.

76 Detail of the reveal of the arch at the entrance. The goffering has a rib-and-interspace motif, here used ornamentally. The marble was not worked until the stone slabs had been laid.

House of the Raja Birbal at Fathepur Sikri, built in 1569
Section, elevation and ground-plan 1:300

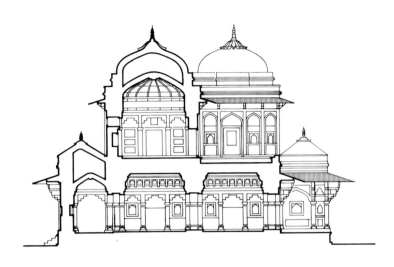

Ground floor

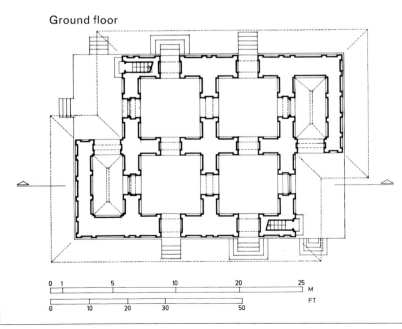

| 0 | 1 | 5 | 10 | 20 | 25 | M |

FT

| 0 | 10 | 20 | 30 | 50 |

Detail of a corbel and section of a geometric structure which is carved in sandstone 1:20

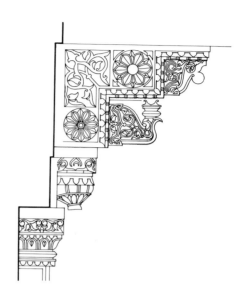

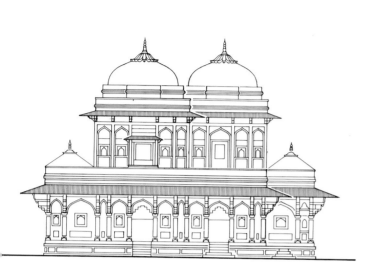

Upper storey

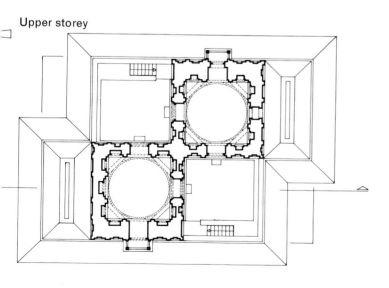

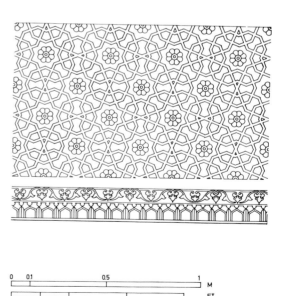

0 0.1   0.5   1
|__|_____|_____| M

0   0.5   1   2   3
|_____|_____|_____|_____| FT

Notes

Bijapur (see grey plan p. 147/148)

Bijapur in Southern India differs from the residences of the Great Mughuls in Northern India even in its layout. The town is an irregular oval in shape and has a citadel in the centre. Some streets pass it, while others link it with the gateways of the town; the irregular course of most of the streets indicates that the town was not laid out on a systematic plan, but grew slowly around the citadel. It lacks all the characteristic features of Hindu town planning which, in accordance with ancient Indian theories on architecture, had to manifest certain geometric relationships. But there are no parallels between Bijapur and Mughul residences either. As a matter of principle every Mughul town was situated on a bend of a river like a sickle, curved in the opposite direction to that in which the river flowed. If, as at Fathepur Sikri, there was no river in the vicinity, the Mughuls at least made an artificial lake on one side of the city. The citadel with its palaces was generally not situated in the centre of the town but directly on the bank of the river or lake.

Bijapur is situated on a level barren plain. This unfavourable location may have caused the sultans, who belonged to the 'Adil Shah dynasty, to surround with fortresses some well-watered hilly ground and to start work here on building a satellite town as large as the capital city.

Supplying a town with enough water for drinking and irrigation purposes was one of the most difficult problems that faced Indian town planners. Fathepur Sikri had to be abandoned as an imperial residence since it was found impossible to maintain a sufficient supply of water. When laying siege to a town the enemy always tried to destroy the canals, the lifelines of the settlement. A greater luxury could hardly be imagined than artificially irrigated gardens and lakes within the palace precinct. The building of waterside palaces was not due to military considerations but for the luxury of possessing water in abundance.

It was 'Adil Shah's wish to transform Bijapur into a paradise of parks and flowers. Two methods of obtaining water were available to him. The local Hindus had for centuries dug wells and so satisfied their very modest needs for water from subterranean sources. But it was not possible to obtain in this way enough water to cultivate the gardens. For this reason dikes were built outside the town, on the north, west and south sides, and the water from the monsoon rains collected in large shallow reservoirs. From these the water flowed throughout the year to the town, situated about four miles away. In addition a subterranean canal carried to Bijapur water from the brooks of Nauraspur, the satellite town already mentioned.

All aqueducts had water-towers and control shafts at regular intervals. Water was admitted into the lower part of these towers and expelled from the upper part. In this way the sediment was removed several times before the water flowed into the thin clay pipes of the municipal distribution system.

A particularly pliant kind of mortar was used by masons at Bijapur for flat plastered ceilings and bowls; from this were also constructed several large watertight reservoirs within the city walls. Only by expenditure on such a scale was it possible to transform this town into a garden city that would endure for several generations.

Today most of the conduits are blocked and many of the gardens dried up. However, when the Archaeological Survey of India began to renovate the most important monument in the town, the Gol Gumbaz, the gardens of this mausoleum were laid out afresh and provided with a system of artificial irrigation.

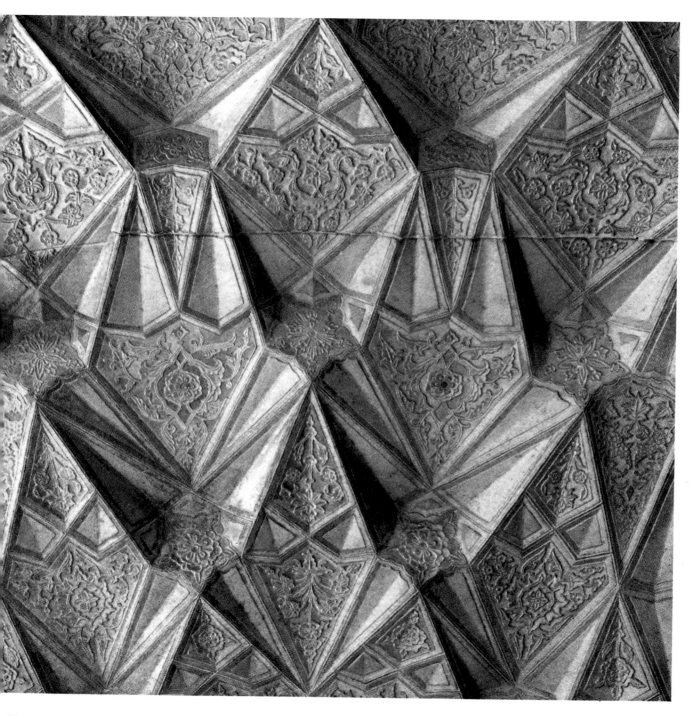

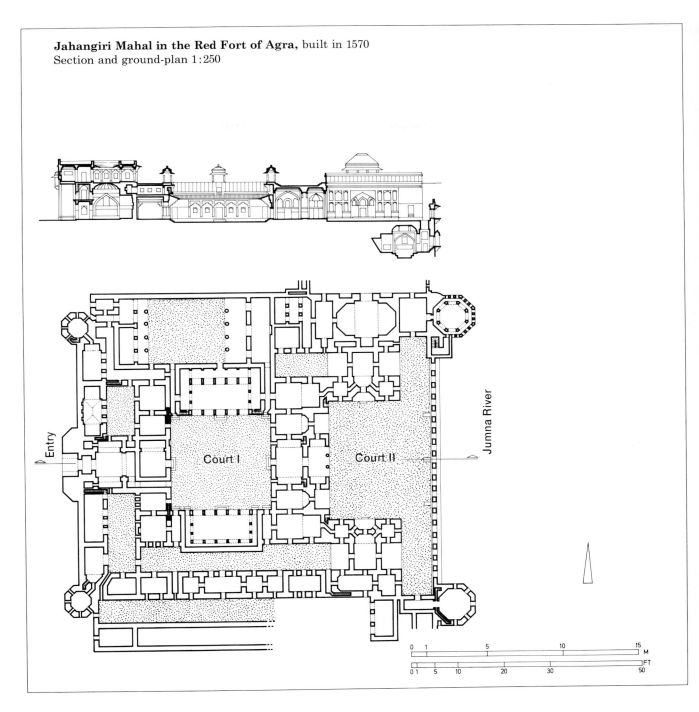

Jahangiri Mahal in the Red Fort of Agra, built in 1570
Section and ground-plan 1:250

Entry

Court I

Court II

Jumna River

0 1   5   10   15 M

0 1 5 10   20   30   50 FT

Humayun's tomb at Delhi, built in 1565
(Architect: Mirak Mirza Ghiyas)
Site plan 1:5000

1 Humayun's tomb
2 Babur's tomb
3 River Jumna
4 Arabic serail
5 Isa Khan's tomb
6 Approach

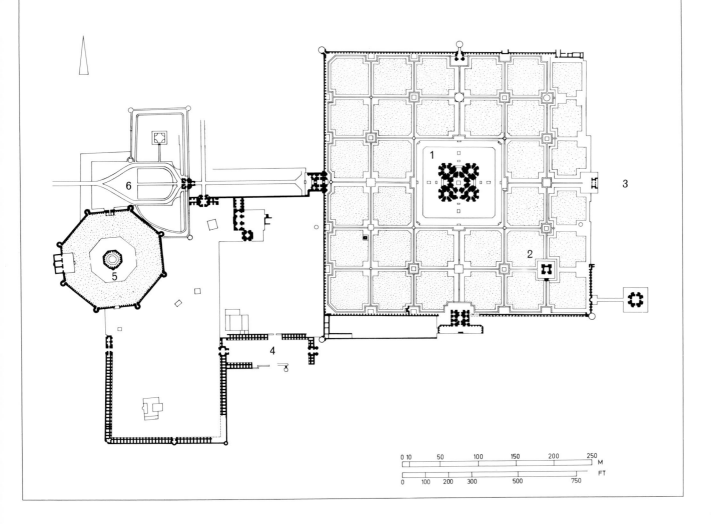

0 10   50   100   150   200   250
                                      M
0   100 200 300   500   750
                                      FT

3. Taj Mahal and Gol Gumbaz

The emperors Jahangir and Shah Jahan tended increasingly to turn away from the traditional Hindu types of building. Humayun's tomb had already ushered in a wave of Islamization, which did far more to oust native types than any Persian influence hitherto exerted. Only the circumstance that Indian craftsmen were far superior to their colleagues in neighbouring lands, particularly in working stone, ensured that some Hindu formal elements would survive in Islamic architecture.

We shall discuss in detail two tombs, the Taj Mahal at Agra, the most important Mughul building in Northern India, and Gol Gumbaz at Bijapur, the culminating achievement of the Indo-Islamic style in Southern India, which evolved independently. Both buildings are distinguished by their unusual size.

Taj Mahal (see grey plan, p. 97–8)

In 1630 Mumtaz Mahal, the favourite wife of Shah Jahan, died. Provisionally she was buried at Burhanpur on the river Tapti. After six months her body was transferred to the piece of land at Agra which the emperor had selected for her mausoleum. The preparation and planning of this building lasted two years. Shah Jahan consulted pictures and designs of all the famous buildings in the world, for he wished this memorial to his late wife to surpass every wonder of his age. But since a Mughul tomb was to be not only a memorial but also a dwelling for the deceased, it was set in a delightful garden. It was not unusual for a ruler to lay out the garden of his own mausoleum during his lifetime and to use it for ceremonial receptions. Already under the Turkish sultans of Delhi it was a common practice to provide a deceased ruler with a complete royal household. Thus Ibn Batuta, the Arab traveller to whom we are indebted for information about the country and its inhabitants in the fourteenth century, gives an account of his employment as administrator of the tomb of Qutb-ud-din:
'The inhabitants of India are in the habit of observing toward the deceased the same ceremonies with which they honoured them during their lifetime. Thus

elephants and horses are brought along and tied to the decorated gate of the mausoleum. I too, when giving my instructions for the tomb of Qutb-ud-din, took into account the custom of the country. I employed 150 readers of the Koran, 80 students and eight Sufis, a precentor, persons to summon the faithful to prayer, readers with particularly fine voices, panegyrists, secretaries to take note of those who did not appear and announcers... I also employed another class of people who were called people of the outer court. These included menials, cooks, messengers, water-carriers, cup-bearers, betel-bearers, bearers of weapons, arrows and sunshades, keepers of the wardrobe, valets and officers of the guard. In all there were 460 persons.'

The splendour described here pales by comparison with the ceremonial at the tomb of Mumtaz Mahal. The broad avenues in the garden of the Taj Mahal and the spacious gateway and guest quarters point to the fact that the emperor and his entire court kept his wife's memory alive.

No reliable account has survived of the competition which Shah Jahan is said to have held before choosing the design, or the name of the architect who was commissioned to carry out the work. Father Manrique, a travelling Augustinian friar, writes that the Venetian jeweller and silversmith Geronimo Verronea supplied the sovereign with the design. Native chronicles, on the other hand, which list all the participants, do not mention the names of any Europeans. But even these Indian chronicles, as Dr Chaghtai's thorough examination in the 1930s has shown, were very unreliable copies of earlier accounts, or even forgeries dating from the eighteenth and nineteenth centuries. They turned up all over the place because Europeans took such a keen interest in the Taj Mahal and because there were no authentic sources. As late as the nineteenth century manuscripts were compiled in which a certain Ustad Isa, about whose origins the authors were in some disagreement, was identified as the architect of the Taj Mahal. Ustad Isa, repeatedly referred to as 'the best architect of his time', may be an imaginary person.

The names of the most important architects of Shah Jahan's reign are known; they appear in trustworthy chronicles as well as in inscriptions on several buildings. There is a Mulla Murshid Shirazi, from Shiraz in Persia as his name implies, who has entered the annals under the title of Mukarrimat Khan. He had already served under Jahangir and was entrusted by Shah Jahan with the task of supervising the building of the Taj Mahal, and later of overseeing construction of the Red Fort at Shahjahanabad. The other overseer who collaborated on equal terms with Mukarrimat Khan at the Taj Mahal was Mir Abdul Karim. He, too, had proved his worth under Jahangir. In his memoirs Jahangir writes:
'As I had made up my mind to proceed to the Deccan, I gave an order to 'Abdu-l-Karim Ma'muri, to go to Mandu and to prepare a new building for my private residence, and to repair the building for my private residence, and repair the buildings of the old kings... On the 28th, as a reward for the buildings of Mandu having been completed through his excellent exertions, I promoted 'Abdu-l-Karim to the rank of 800 personal and 400 horse, and dignified him with the title of Ma'mur Khan (the architect-Khan)[6].'
But Mamur Khan's connection with the Taj Mahal is limited to his activity as a practising architect.

Luft Allah, the son of an architect named Ahmad who enjoyed high esteem at that time, relates in a poem that his father built the Taj Mahal and the Fort at Delhi. So far as Delhi is concerned, this statement is confirmed by two authentic chronicles, the 'Badsha Nama' and the 'Amal Saleh'. But this claim to have designed the Taj Mahal finds no support elsewhere. Only the fact that – according to an inscription on the tomb of Dilras Banu Rabi'a-ud-Daurani – another son of Ahmad, Ata-Ullah, was the architect of this reduced copy of the Taj Mahal at Aurangabad could be taken as evidence that Ahmad did in fact collaborate in building the Taj Mahal.

Finally, we have Ali Mardan Khan. He had renounced the viceregal throne at Kandahar, to which he was entitled, and had come to Shah Jahan's court at Lahore, where he laid various architectural projects before the emperor; these were implemented and made him famous. His first masterpiece in India was a conduit through which water was carried from the upper reaches of the river Ravi into the palace to water the Shalimar gardens; his second masterpiece was the completion of a canal which made the palace at Delhi independent of the city's inadequate water supply. However, since he was chiefly a builder of canals and bridges, Ali Mardan may be ruled out as a possible architect of the Taj Mahal.

The emperor's architectural talents are repeatedly mentioned in the sources. In 1619, when he was still Prince Khurram, he travelled to Kashmir for the first time with Jahangir and surprised his father by his exceptionally keen interest in architecture. Thereupon Jahangir entrusted him with the design and supervision of the Shalimar gardens at Srinagar. The direct influence later exerted by Shah Jahan as emperor upon the architecture of his domains is mentioned in one chronicle.
'Occasionally His Majesty supervised the work of goldsmiths, jewellers and sculptors. Thereupon specialists commissioned to design new buildings would submit their plans to His Majesty, who discussed them with expert persons. He knew that sumptuous, splendid monuments would serve to immortalize his reign; he knew that they would provide a vivid testimony to the age in which they were erected. For this reason the state encouraged building work, so that everything might be executed in the most exquisite manner. Various monuments, which even the best-versed architect could not have devised, were drawn up by His Majesty personally. His advice or his objections were regarded as binding. Everything that had been definitely settled, in any manner whatsoever, was passed on to the artists by 'the right hand man of the empire', who also added His Majesty's explanations or recommendations. In this way the architect and the official in charge of the construction work always found it easy to agree. In tranquil times the work of the ministry of public buildings became so extensive that even the most critical observers, the artists and the best engineers, were deeply impressed with the achievements of that era,

which the author has already mentioned in many different contexts.'

Havell, one of the best known interpreters of Indian art, has endeavoured to prove in various publications that the Taj Mahal was a purely Hindu monument. He points in particular to the fact that the grouping of four small kiosks around the large false dome can be derived directly from the Hindu 'panch-ratna' ('five jewels') temple plan. Indeed it was already common for theological reasons to erect in Northern India, long before the Muslim invasion, four small cells around the huge temple sanctuary in the corners of a large platform (cf. the example of Bhubanesvar in the companion volume on Hindu and Buddhist art in India). The weakness of this comparison lies in the

Ground-plan of the Hesht Bihisht, garden pavilion at Isfahan, 17th century, which has affinities with that of the Taj Mahal

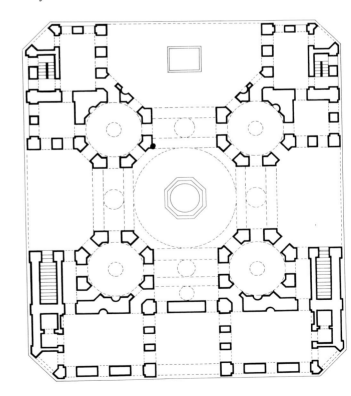

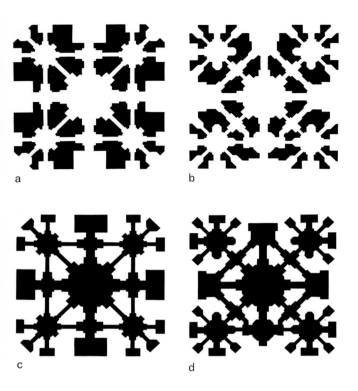

a

b

c

d

Ground-plans of the Taj Mahal and Humayun's tomb

a) areas filled with masonry in the Taj Mahal
b) areas filled with masonry in Humayun's tomb
c) interior spaces in the Taj Mahal
d) interior spaces in Humayun's tomb

fact that the kiosks of the Taj Mahal cannot have been the starting-point of the design, but instead were merely the spatial consequences of the model preferred by Islamic rulers for monuments as well as gardens (cf. the garden of the Taj Mahal with the Hayat Bakhsh Bagh in the Red Fort at Delhi, and the chapter on 'gardens of the Mughuls'). This model may have originated in Persia. The garden pavilion of Hasht Bihisht ('seven paradises') at Isfahan, although built as late as 1670, i.e. after the Taj Mahal, may be mentioned here as an example of these Persian ground-plans.

One prototype of the Taj Mahal was Humayun's tomb. Although the two mausolea differ in size (the Taj Mahal is some 57 metres deep, as against 48 metres for Humayun's tomb), the ground-plans may here be juxtaposed on the same scale for the purposes of comparison.

In sacred Hindu texts it was laid down that dwellings were only to consist of perishable material such as bamboo, wood or clay; temples, on the other hand, as images of a temporally limitless universe were supposed to be built of a durable material, namely stone. For a variety of reasons the Hindus preferred a monolithic rock-cut temple to a monument constructed of ashlar masonry. Even at the beginning of the second millennium A.D., when for practical reasons the temple made of cut stones had already asserted itself, architects still emulated specifically monolithic types of chamber and modes of working. The Hindu ideal of massiveness in architecture, of a monolithic tower or cosmic mountain with a small chamber in the centre, exerted an influence even upon Mughul architects, as the tombs of Humayun and Mumtaz Mahal illustrate.

When the Hindus hewed narrow corridors and chambers out of huge monoliths they did not leave any walls, such as were to be found in brick buildings, but instead left large masses of rock, to which they attached the same formal importance as to the corridors and chambers hewn between them. In Humayun's tomb we encounter one of the first monumental syntheses between Hindu massive architecture and the Persian sequence of rooms.

Let us also consider the vertical section of the Taj Mahal and Humayun's tomb: in both cases the main hall is crowned by a flat dome; in both cases a void is found between the inner and outer shells of the dome; in both cases the domes project over the edge of the drum – in Humayun's tomb only very slightly, but in the Taj Mahal already to a greater extent. Overhanging domes are ridiculous when built of stone. Unless they are supported or braced by some kind of artifice, the horizontal thrust would force them asunder. The bulbous shape conforms to the principles applicable to architecture in wood. It was first executed in Central Asia, whence it reached Asia Minor; here it was applied on a grand scale in the Omayyad mosque at Damascus. Of Timur it is known that on all his campaigns through Asia he categorically instructed his officers to spare the lives of artists and artisans, who were then deported to Samarkand. Here, with the collaboration of Syrian and Persian craftsmen, arose the most important monument in that city, a mosque which, after Timur had been interred in it, was given the name of Gur Amir ('tomb of the Amir').

It would be inappropriate to associate the domes of Gur Amir, the tomb at Delhi and the Taj Mahal were it not for the fact that all three are false domes. The

Section of the Gur-Amir, Timur's tomb at Samarkand

buildings also resemble one another in a different respect: there is a sepulchre beneath the main chamber. The crypt of Gur Amir was only hollowed out later, when the mosque was transformed into a mausoleum. Several years after this reconstruction a descendant of Timur donated a replica of the sarcophagus, which was placed in the main chamber. The reason for producing a cenotaph of this kind was probably to encourage popular veneration of the deceased, without exposing the tomb directly to contact with the mass of the common people. The double dome, subterranean sepulchral chamber and the replica of the sarcophagus in the main chamber, were all features that the Indians adopted as fixed components of a monumental royal tomb.

The outline of the dome of Humayun's tomb is borrowed from Persian prototypes; and the exceptionally high drum of the Taj Mahal also recalls Persian monuments or the Gur Amir. Is it at all possible that knowledge of the Gur Amir could have reached Agra? Shah Jahan never went to Samarkand, but the 'Amal Saleh' chronicle refers to the fact that the Gur Amir not only was familiar to him but even had a certain significance for him, although this point is not elucidated. We are told only that for some unknown reason the emperor once sent one and a half lakhs of rupees, i.e. 150,000 rupees, to Samarkand 'for the guardians of the tomb of Sahib Quiram Timur'. Although the reason for this handsome gift cannot be discovered, there can be no doubt that there was some connection between Agra and Samarkand.

The chain of prototypes of the Taj Mahal, which starts with the Omayyad mosque in Damascus and passes by way of the Gur Amir in Samarkand to Humayun's tomb, ends with a small tomb at Delhi, to which we may now turn. This is the mausoleum of Khan Khanan, a son of Bairam Khan. Khan Khanan died in 1626, and his tomb lies chronologically somewhere between that of Humayun and the Taj Mahal. In several details it is possible to make out that it was modelled on Humayun's tomb. On the other hand, there is also a staggering similarity between its façades and those of the Taj Mahal. The architect was

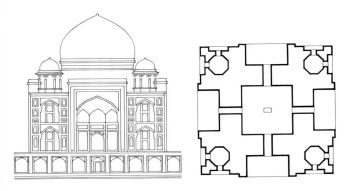

Khan Khanan's tomb at Delhi. The façades were taken as a model by the architect of the Taj Mahal

obviously trying to avoid several shortcomings in the spatial arrangement of Humayun's tomb, especially the resolution of the entire complex into four corner buildings and the ensuing excessive distance between the kiosks on the roof and the main dome. Without abandoning the graphic treatment of the building, derived from Persian prototypes, attention was again turned to fifteenth-century monuments. The façades of these tombs were articulated in the following way: in the axes were tall portals, flanked by two smaller niches, one on top of the other. In order to avoid disintegration, the architect fell back on the idea of the masonry cube, in which the portals are not set back like those of Humayun's tomb but actually project forward a little from the façade. The building thus looks more compact than its forerunner, particularly as the contours of the kiosks on the roof blend with the large sphere in the centre, as the corner buildings have been moved closer together. By extending the drum slightly the main dome was prevented from sinking entirely from view between the ancillary cupolas.

The architect of the Taj Mahal obviously did not want to create something novel or sensational, but only to come a stage closer to the ideal type of tomb, following the well mapped course of the Indo-Islamic architectural tradition. Humayun's tomb forms the thesis and Khan Khanan's tomb the antithesis; from

this evolved the synthesis of the Taj Mahal, which combines the merits of both monuments.

The reasons that led the architect of Khan Khanan's tomb to abandon the octagonal ground-plan were no doubt known to the architect of the Taj Mahal, but he also saw that the rectangular positioning of the façades containing niches had produced too hard a solution at the corners. His answer to the problem was to cut off the corners of the building according to. the so-called octagon-baghdadi, while letting each individual façade develop on its own plane!

Now there is no doubt that a body of masonry such as the Taj Mahal or Khan Khanan's tomb stands out somewhat abruptly and isolated against the surrounding plain, on account of its great elevation, adopted from earlier monuments, though the effect of this is limited by giving it two storeys. Shah Jahan, who in all his palaces was concerned to emphasize the impression of space, and in whose buildings there was no climax that did not have its introduction or epilogue, incorporated this mausoleum into ancillary buildings situated axially to one another, so that by contrast to all earlier tombs the outline of the Taj Mahal forms part of a rhythmic undulating total effect.

New emphases were added by the minarets at the corners of the platform, which neither belong to the main building nor can be considered as ancillary buildings. These are enlarged versions of the small minarets which were already employed in Humayun's tomb, which were featured on the gateways to Akbar's tomb as massive towers, without any real relationship to the building itself, and finally which mark off the corners of a flat building, Jahangir's tomb near Lahore, where they have the size of real mosque minarets. This flat building and the minarets seemed to the emperor to be the right kind of framework for the mausoleum of Mumtaz Mahal.

Twentieth-century architecture will go down into history under the motto 'form corresponds to func-

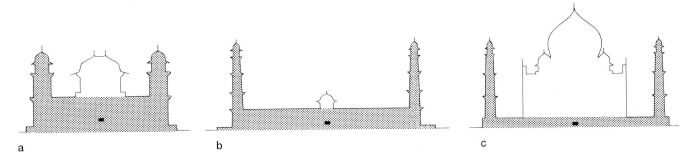

Three Mughul mausolea with structural affinities

a) I'timad-ud-daula's tomb at Agra
b) Jahangir's tomb near Lahore
c) Mumtaz Mahal's tomb, called the Taj Mahal, at Agra

tion'. From a modern point of view it is particularly difficult to feel certain about a phenomenon such as the false or double dome. It is hard for us to see why the chamber of Humayun's tomb would appear less harmonious if it were to extend as far as the outer shell of the dome; we also find it objectionable that in the Taj Mahal, the largest of all the chambers – the space between the inner and outer shells of the dome – should be inaccessible and therefore unserviceable. It fulfils no function in the shaping of the interior and is there solely because the building had to have a certain exterior outline. The external shape has no readily understandable connection with the interior. Under the influence of Hindu architecture, which was emphatically non-tectonic, the Islamic buildings in India turned into monumental sculptures.

Stages in design of ground-plan of the Taj Mahal (reconstruction)

Dieulafoy's study of Persian monuments mentioned above shows that many tombs and mosques are based in their general layout and in matters of detail upon a proportional framework. Dieulafoy has proved that in Persia use was made above all of the circle, square and equilateral triangle, in order to bring all parts of the building into a harmonious relationship. The same geometric figures also determined the measurements of Hindu temples. Thus in Mughul architecture we find two traditions, each of which attached great importance to the geometric relationship. Is it not probable that the architect of the Taj Mahal – whichever tradition he was closer to – also followed strictly geometric forms? A few exercises with a pair of compasses will suffice to reconstruct the geometric framework employed.

Stage 1: A basic circle was drawn around M, the point where two axes intersect at right angles. Circles

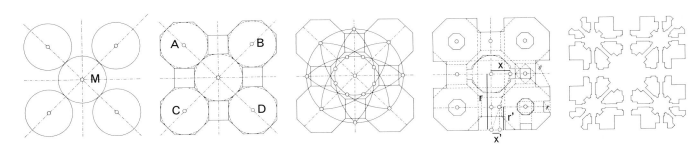

with the same radius, situated on the diagonals, are drawn tangentially to the basic circle.

Stage 2: An octagon is circumscribed around each circle, producing the octagonal structure that frequently serves Islamic architects also as the basic structure for pierced stone lattices. The octagons in the corners indicate the point at which the corners of the building are to be sited; the one in the centre indicates the size of the interior, including its niches.

Stage 3: Points A, B, C and D form the centres of the corner rooms. If arcs are drawn with the radii AB, BC etc. around A, B, C and D, we obtain the size of the interior, excluding the niches.

Stage 4: The protracted sides of a square inscribed in the octagonal interior yield the width of the niches of the portal; their depth results from the position of the small squares situated between the octagons. These squares contain the vestibules, the sides of which are formed by bisecting one side of the square.

The size of the small corner rooms is given by $r : x = r' : x'$; similarly, the width of the niches of their portals is given by the protracted sides of the inscribed squares, and their depth by the proportion between the large niches of the axial portals.

Stage 5: Corridors running along all the axes complete this scheme of the Taj Mahal's ground-plan.

Since an observer can only take in the axes of a building if they are directly related to its centre, off-centre diagonal axes were avoided in the Taj Mahal. The scheme of the ground-plan is thus clearer than that of Humayun's tomb. Anyone walking through the building can work out at any given moment his position in relation to the clearly identifiable network of axes. If, on the other hand, one were to stand in one of the off-centre diagonal corridors of Humayun's tomb, one would be in no optical relationship to the principal centre.

In the Taj Mahal it is possible at any time for a visitor to make out his 'relative' standpoint in regard to the ground-plan; however, it is certainly not possible for him to ascertain his 'absolute' standpoint. One cannot know whether one is in the east, west, south or north wing. This shortcoming pertains to all buildings which – in relation to two axes running vertically to one another – are absolutely symmetrical. Hindu architects were already aware of this when they built square temple towers. For this reason they distinguished one of the four façades by adding a gateway or a projecting row of columns – usually on the east side, as the cella was entered from the east. This slight deviation from absolute symmetry not only accentuated the entrance but also indicated to the faithful, as they proceeded around the monument in the rite of 'pradakshina', at which moment they had completed one or more circumambulations.

In Northern India the development of medieval temple architecture led architects to move the 'pradakshina' into the interior of the temple, where it formed a circular corridor. Circumambulation, as a symbol of worship, is a custom practised both by Buddhists and Hindus. The peoples of the Arabian desert also knew the rite of circumambulation, which they called 'tawaf'. Already before the time of Muhammad it was common practice to walk seven times round sacred magic stones, of which the most famous is the Ka'ba in Mecca, in order to partake of the power latent in the stone.

Gol Gumbaz, the tomb of Muhammad 'Adil Shah
(see grey plan, p. 148)

The Muslim architects did not confine their vigorous building programme to Northern India. In some sultanates of Southern India there flourished a school of Indo-Islamic architecture, independent of that in the north, which continued to develop until the Southern Indian kingdoms were annexed by the Mughul empire. The most powerful opponent of Shah Jahan in Southern India was Sultan Muhammad of Bijapur (1626–1656), a descendant of the Turkish dynasty of the 'Adil Shahi.

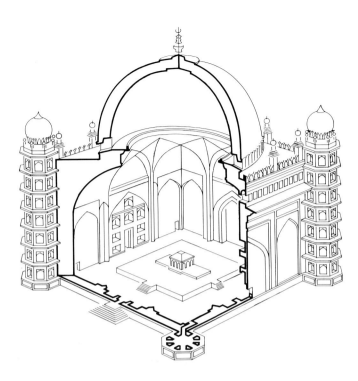

Gol Gumbaz at Bijapur, built between 1626 and 1656: cut-away diagram to show lines of perspective

From the very outset of his reign this ruler pursued the ambitious plan of building for himself a mausoleum which in size and splendour was to overshadow not only the ostentatious tombs of his ancestors but also every other monument in India. His thirty-year reign did not suffice to carry out the detailed work on all the vast wall surfaces of the so-called Gol Gumbaz ('round dome'). Its unfinished state makes the building look less elegant than its forerunners. Neither the grey basalt with which it was faced nor its walls, decorated with a coat of plaster, can match the wealth of materials and forms one finds in Northern Indian buildings.

Only the Turkish lineage of the ruler and some of his artisans can explain why in the isolation of the Deccan a dome should have been built that is roughly

as large as that of the Pantheon or St. Peter's in Rome (which was built later), and is larger than that of Santa Sophia in Constantinople.

On entering the spacious square interior below the plain dome, the visitor is dumbfounded by its size but inevitably disappointed at the disproportion between the vast expenditure of effort and the undifferentiated treatment. There is no vestibule to prepare one for the surprise one experiences on entering the great chamber; outside as well as inside one lacks the sense of scale necessary to relate the building to a human dimension. Thus, for example, it is impossible, either from the gallery at the base of the dome or from the floor of the hall, to take in every feature of the great spherical space above one, plunged as it is in a grey twilight, or to measure the distance visually.

In the Taj Mahal, too, it is not possible to make out the scale of the inner shell of the dome over the sepulchral chamber. In both cases the viewer is left guessing as to whether the hall is closed off at the top by a hemisphere or merely has a flat curvature. In the Taj Mahal this does not affect one's impression of the space, since one's eye is directed to the filigree work of the windows and the trellis work surrounding the cenotaph. In the Gol Gumbaz, on the other hand, one can observe how visitors on entering immediately look upward, full of expectation; they are then overcome by uncertainty when they see – or rather, have to imagine – an empty hemispherical shell.

In comparing the Gol Gumbaz with other tombs built by rulers of the same dynasty, one is struck by the fact that it bears similarities to its predecessors in its ground-plan and that all the differences are to be found exclusively in the elevation. It seems particularly surprising that the basement of the Gol Gumbaz has an inner circular wall (M), which has the same dimensions as the outer circular wall (N) that absorbs the entire weight of the dome (see grey plan, p. 148). What purpose do these massive inner foundations serve? They support only a thin ceiling and an insignificant wooden pavilion over the cenotaph!

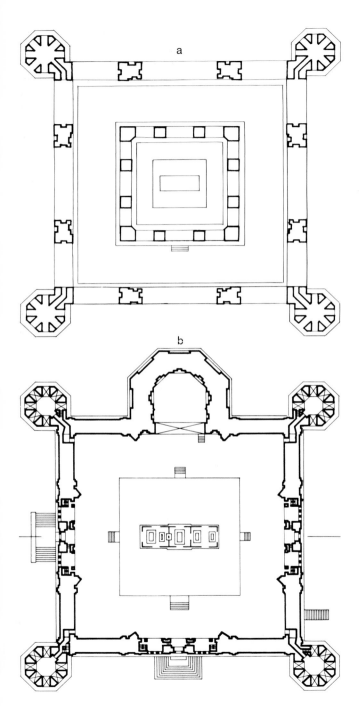

a

b

Comparison of Jahan Begum's tomb (a) and Gol Gumbaz (b), both planned by Sultan Muhammad 'Adil Shah of Bijapur

The solution to this puzzle is to be found in another building. Just as Shah Jahan, when building the Taj Mahal, dreamed of erecting a second mausoleum of the same kind for himself on the other bank of the Jumna, so Muhammad 'Adil Shah wanted to build for his consort, Jahan Begum, a copy of the Gol Gumbaz a few miles east of Bijapur. Its ground-plan bears a resemblance to that of the Gol Gumbaz in many details, such as the separation of the towers at the corners; the dimensions, too, are the same. Only in one point do the two ground-plans differ: there is a row of pillars leading off directly above the massive inner circle of the foundations of Jahan Begum's tomb. Although only the lowermost courses of this mausoleum were completed, the pilasters indicate that its upper part was intended to assume the form traditional for a tomb. As in its prototypes, the dome was to have been supported by an inner set of walls, laid out on a square plan, and a low arcade was to enclose the main chamber. An example of this structure is the tomb of Sultan Ibrahim, Muhammad's father. The dome of Jahan Begum's tomb, resting on the pillars of the inner circle, was intended to differ from that of the Gol Gumbaz by its smaller size. The pillars of the outer circle on each side supported three low arches with a wide span, such as had been constructed shortly beforehand in Bijapur, on the model of the Gulbarga mosque.

The massive inner circle of the foundations of the Gol Gumbaz leads to the only possible conclusion that in this case, too, the original plan provided for a smaller domed chamber, surrounded by an open arcade. It was not until the foundations had been completed that the sultan (or the architect) hit upon the idea of resting the dome upon the outer walls and thereby enlarging its volume several times over.

In 1615 Sultan Ibrahim II completed the Ibrahim Rauza ('tomb of Ibrahim'), which we have mentioned above. An inscription on the north door of the sepul-

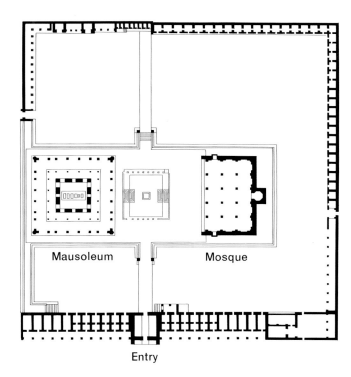

Mausoleum

Mosque

Entry

Site plan of the Ibrahim Rauza at Bijapur, 17th century

marble and red sandstone) or the ornamentation (here plaster, there 'pietra dura' inlay in the late Moghul style), one will come to the conclusion that the monuments at Bijapur have a provincial look about them. One reason for this may be that the distant sultanates of Southern India had no direct contact with neighbouring cultures. Mutual contact between India, Central Asia and Persia brought a constant stream of artists with new ideas to the court of the Great Mughuls. In Southern India, on the other hand, craftsmen who had immigrated from Turkey found themselves in a Hindu environment which exerted an ever stronger influence upon the appearance of their monuments. Here the encounter of two architectural traditions often led to compromises and only rarely to a felicitous synthesis, as happened in Northern India.

No Indo-Islamic monument lacks homogeneity of form and structure to the same degree as does the Ibrahim Rauza. Consider the section: above the tomb chamber there is a heavy and oppressive flat ceiling

Section of the Ibrahim Rauza (tomb of Ibrahim) at Bijapur

chral chamber gives the date of its construction in the form of a chronogram:
'Full of admiration, the heavens watched as this house was built and one could say that a second heaven appeared as it sprang from the earth. The garden of paradise borrowed its beauty from this garden. Every single column is here as graceful as cypresses in the garden of purity. An angel of heaven announced the date when it was completed in the following words: This edifice, which fills men's hearts with joy, is dedicated to the memory of Taj Sultana.'

Nineteenth-century art historians were full of praise for the beauty of the Ibrahim Rauza; some were even disposed to place this building on an equal footing with the Mughul monuments of Northern India. If one merely compares the materials used (here mean-looking dusty grey basalt, there bright white

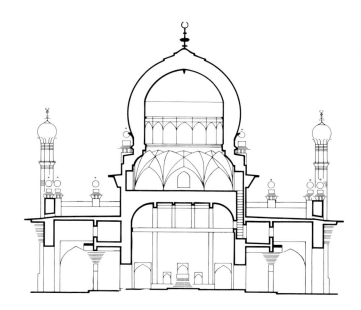

of Hindu origin; above this, without any spatial connection, we find a typical Islamic vaulted area which extends all the way up to the dome and can be reached only by way of a narrow flight of steps. As in the Taj Mahal, the largest chamber in the interior is unused! A similar juxtaposition of Hindu and Islamic elements, as in the flat ceiling and dome, i.e. the lower and upper chamber, is also found in the surrounding arcade. On the outside it is closed off by pointed arches; in the interior some wholly Hindu pillars with corbelling and architraves support a small gallery inserted in between. The contrast between the arcades and the corbelled constructions is a harsh one.

From our sketch of the layout it can be seen that Ibrahim's tomb is not constructed symmetrically, as was that of Mumtaz Mahal. One enters the square courtyard through an off-centre door on the north side. The axis of the building, which runs vertically to that of the entrance, is likewise off-centre. It has not yet been ascertained whether the division of the square exactly in accordance with the Golden Section is based upon a geometric construction, or whether this harmonious division was worked out instinctively, without any knowledge of the Golden Section. The asymmetry helped to avoid a conflict such as was encountered by the architects of the Taj Mahal: where, in a symmetrical layout, should the mosque be placed? In the case of the Taj Mahal there was only one possible solution: to erect, in correspondence to the mosque, which was situated on the western side, a building in the same shape on the eastern side of the mausoleum. In the asymmetrical Ibrahim Rauza a dummy of this kind was not necessary. Tomb and prayer-hall were clearly co-ordinated, one on the left and the other on the right of the visitor as he entered the building.

The tomb is square in plan and is oriented towards the sarcophagus in the centre. The mosque is a building with no focal point in the interior, since its purpose is to point toward the centre of Islam to the west. Accordingly it is not square in ground-plan. But since the platform on which the two elements of the building stand measures the same width on either side of the axis of the entrance, an area remained empty in front of the mosque. This was used to good purpose as an assembly-place for the faithful.

The lavish ornamentation of all buildings during this period, as well as the strikingly plastic treatment of many architectural elements, may be interpreted as the product of Hindu influence.

As further proof that Hindu architects continued to exert an influence upon the architecture of Bijapur, we may mention that at no stage of development was there any question of giving up the traditional 'chayas' supported by brackets. In seventeenth-century Mughul architecture the circle of brackets was ousted by a marble cavetto. At this time the method of corbelled construction reached a climax in Southern India at the Gol Gumbaz. It not only boasted the largest dome in India but excelled over all other buildings in another respect: its corbelled cornice, which projected outward for a distance of over 3 metres, was the largest in the world.

The Mughul Gardens

In the Koran paradise is described as a celestial garden in which the righteous are surrounded by every conceivable kind of luxury. A finer concept of paradise there could hardly have been for the Arab peoples, surrounded as they were by hostile deserts and dependent upon a few fertile oases for their livelihood. In Persia, too, where the prototypes of the Mughul gardens are to be sought, most of the land was barren, and it required much effort to irrigate the orchards and flower gardens of the palaces. It was upon irrigation that the existence of gardens depended in Arabia, Persia and India; and it was the irrigation system that gave the garden its form. So-called 'Hanging Gardens' existed already in Babylon; the irrigated terraces of Persepolis were constructed in emulation of these.

Hindus and Buddhists worshipped certain trees and flowers, but there was no horticulture in India before the Muslim invasion. Firuz Shah records that in the fourteenth century he laid out 'one hundred gardens'

In his memoirs Babur states that Akbar had two miniatures painted of the Bagh-e-wafa (Garden of Fidelity)

around his residence. None of them have survived. The first impulse to the great development of horticulture in the sixteenth century was given by Babur, the first Mughul emperor. His native state of Ferghana kept alive the traditions of the Persian terraced garden, described by one Persian author of the time in the following words:

'Wherever possible, the Persians lay out gardens on an even slope. The garden I shall describe was constructed in such a way that two courses of crystal-clear water met before a building, forming a large lake in which countless swans, geese and ducks disported themselves. Below this lake were seven waterfalls—as many as there are planets. And below these waterfalls again was a second small lake and a splendid gateway decorated with blue tiles. The reader may think that this was all; but no, for not only from the lake but also between the waterfalls jets of water spouted up so high into the air that the spray, as it descended, was like a rain of diamonds. How often was I moved by the rippling of the fountains and the murmuring of the brook as it streamed downhill, over the terraces of the garden, hemmed in by rose bushes, willows, plane-trees, acacias, cypresses and other trees. And I cried with sheer joy until the exceeding beauty and the rushing of the water rocked me to sleep. By Allah, I do believe that the beauty of this garden is unsurpassed even by the garden mentioned in the Koran, of which it is said: The garden of Iram is embellished with tall pillars. Nothing matching it was created in this world.'

In his memoirs Babur time and again describes the climatic conditions, plants and animals which he came across on his campaigns. After he had conquered the empire of Hindustan, he remarked disappointedly: 'Though Hindustan contains so many provinces, none of them has any artificial canals for irrigation. It is watered only by rivers, though in some places, too, there is standing water. Even in those cities which are so situated as to admit of digging a water-course, and thereby bringing water into them, yet no water has been brought in. There may be several reasons for this. One of them is, that water is not absolutely requisite for the crops and the gardens. The autumnal crop is nourished by the rains and the rainy season. It is remarkable that there is a spring crop even though no rain falls. They raise water for the young trees, till they are one or two years old, by means of a water-wheel or buckets; after that time it is not at all necessary to water them... Beside their rivers and standing waters, they have some running water in their ravines and hollows; they have no aqueducts or canals in their gardens or palaces. In their buildings they study neither elegance nor climate, appearance nor regularity[7].'

As soon as Babur felt sure of his hold on the country he had conquered, he began to lay out a garden on the bank of the river Jumna. The chief purpose of this garden was to alleviate the intolerable heat in this territory by making use of extensive stretches of water and shady trees. Already in the first few days of his invasion many of his soldiers had been stricken by the heat, 'as though a poisonous breath had touched them'. The garden at Agra was the model upon which all later parks were based; a similar one was laid out by Babur near Kabul as early as 1508. The so-called 'Garden of Fidelity' at Kabul already possessed all the features of the great Mughul gardens. Emperor Akbar, when he compiled his grandfather's memoirs, caused a miniature to be painted in a Persian manuscript after his description of this garden.

'Opposite to the fort of Adinapur, to the south [of Kabul], on a rising ground, I formed a char-bagh (or great garden), in the year nine hundred and fourteen... I brought plantains and planted them here. They grew and thrived. The year before I had also planted the sugar-cane in it, which throve remarkably well... In the garden there is a small hillock, from which a stream of water, sufficient to drive a mill, incessantly flows into the garden below. The fourfold field-plot of this garden is situated on this eminence. On the south-west part of this garden is a reservoir of water, ten gaz square, which is wholly planted round with orange trees; there are likewise pomegranates. All around the piece of water the ground is quite covered with clover. This spot is the very eye of the beauty of the garden. At the time when the orange becomes yellow, the prospect is delightful. Indeed the garden is charmingly laid out[8].'

Several years later, when the emperor once again spent some time at Kabul, he noted in his diary: 'Next morning I reached the Bagh-e-wafa; it was the season when the garden was in all its glory. Its grass-plots were all covered with clover; its pomegranate trees were entirely of a beautiful yellow colour. It was then the pomegranate season, and the pomegranates were hanging red on the trees. The orange trees were green and cheerful, loaded with innumerable oranges; but the best oranges were not yet ripe. Its pomegranates are excellent, though not equal to the fine ones of our country. I never was so much pleased with the Bagh-e-wafa (the Garden of Fidelity), as on this occasion[9].'

In Europe many parks are merely a stretch of country which is encouraged to develop naturally. In English parks the wilderness sometimes reaches up to the very walls of the house. In France the parts of the garden close to a chateau are treated in an architectonic manner, while those situated further away effect a transition to uncultivated nature. Indian parks are connected with the buildings they belong to much more closely than is the case anywhere in Europe. In the dry climate of Northern India they can only exist as the artificial creation of man and they need particular care. The necessity of irrigating them continually leads to a rigid geometric division by a network of channels and the use of terraces to break up a slope. The formal homogeneity of buildings and gardens is emphasized by the use of the same material to pave paths and face buildings. Moreover, the paths are set at a high level, so that the channels running along them are situated above the flower-beds to be watered, and have outlets for this purpose along the sides. White marble paths lead through gay flower-beds; flowers and precious stones recur as inlay in the marble walls of the palaces.

Early gardens in the Near Eastern empires were mostly designed in conformity with some mystic idea or geometric symbolism. The Hanging Gardens of Persia with their eight terraces symbolize the eight-fold division of Paradise as described in the Koran; the septempartite division is related to the seven planets. Of all the possible subdivisions it was the 'char-bagh' ('four gardens') which characteristically enough predominated in India. Its two axes oriented towards the four cardinal points and its basic square form fitted in exactly with Hindu cosmology. If we did not know that Babur had already laid out a char-bagh at Kabul before he conquered Hindustan, we would be tempted to see this design as the invention of Hindu rather than Islamic architects.

Already in the design of ancient Indian cities we find the same quadripartite division, with each caste being allotted its own specific quarter. As early as the second millennium B.C. Aryan villages were already built in the form of a St. Andrew's cross, at the centre of which stood the tree under which the elders met. This image of the cosmic axis reappears in Buddhist architecture, as a stepped 'honorary umbrella', as well as in the Hindu temples of Southern India, as a cella standing on a small island in a square lake. From this it was but a modest step to the classical Indo-Islamic char-bagh complex. The axial streets had waterways; in the middle of the lake stood the 'baradari', an open water pavilion modelled on the Persian prototype; the garden was enclosed by a high wall such as surrounds all large Hindu temples. The place of the pavilion may be taken by a mausoleum. The first such monumental garden containing a tomb is the one surrounding Humayun's mausoleum in Delhi. Each hedge and each tree serves to accentuate the square network of waterways.

The question now arises how the water was made to flow through a level garden with square symmetrical sides. Let us consider the ground-plan of the garden surrounding Humayun's tomb (see grey plan, p. 78). Would the spring rise in the middle of the square and the water flow down in all directions? Or would the network of waterways be fed from all sides and slope inwards to the centre? In reality neither one method nor the other was adopted. The terrain had to slope southwards. Even though the difference of altitude was minimal, hardly perceptible to the eye, it enabled the water to flow ceaselessly and could also be utilized to make little waterfalls or marble water chutes, the so-called 'chadars'. 'Chadar' (literally, 'shawl') means the white foaming and sloping stretches of water formed between the upper and lower channels by steepening the incline of the vertical waterways that linked them. 'Chadars' of this kind are found in every Mughul garden.

A modern irrigation system could only temporarily stop such vast lawns from becoming scorched by the blazing sun. A genuine Mughul garden, forming an architectonic unit with the mausoleum, could not be

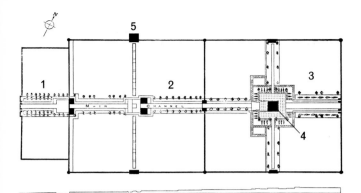

Shalimar Bagh, laid out on a slope at Srinagar (Kashmir), beginning of 17th century

1. Public Garden
2. Emperor's Garden
3. Women's Garden
4. Pavilion
5. Baths

maintained today, for the simple reason that it would need too much water. As a result the harsh silhouette of the building and the vigorous design of the white inlay work in the red sandstone stand in too sharp a contrast to the green lawns. It was originally envisaged that above a gay swirling mass of flowers, fruit-trees and fountains, situated at several levels, the white dome of the tomb should shine forth, supported by the façades with their red and white casing; in this way there would be a masterly transition from the many-coloured diversity of the garden to the simple symbolism of the marble dome.

During the hot summer months the imperial family were in the habit of retiring to the cool of the high-lying Vale of Kashmir in the Himalayas.

Bernier, a seventeenth-century French traveller, who halted for a rest in one of the smaller gardens in Kashmir, relates:
'Achiavel [Achibal], formerly a country house of the kings of Kashemire and now of the Great Mogol. What principally constitutes the beauty of this place is a fountain, whose waters disperse themselves into a hundred canals round the house, which is by no means unseemly, and throughout the gardens. The spring gushes out of the earth with violence, as if it

issued from the bottom of the well, and the water is so abundant that it ought rather to be called a river than a fountain. It is excellent water, and as cold as ice. The garden is very handsome, laid out in regular walks, and full of fruit trees – apple, pear, plum, apricot, and cherry. Jets d'eau in various forms and fish ponds are in great numbers, and there is a cascade which in its fall takes the form and colour of a large sheet, thirty or forty paces in length, producing the finest effect imaginable; especially at night, when innumerable lamps, fixed in parts of the wall adapted for that purpose, are lighted under this sheet of water[10].'

The largest and best known Mughul garden in Kashmir is the Shalimar Bagh ('Garden of the Halls of Love') at Srinagar. It consists of two char-baghs; each square is a self-sufficient entity, separated from the other by a crack in the earth. By way of a front garden, accessible to the public, one enters the lower square. It was here that the ruler and his closest counsellors lived. Along the north side is a bath-house, enlarged to accommodate the small royal household, should the Great Mughul spend several days here. The raised part of the garden is called the 'Women's Garden'.

Shalimar Bagh, the Emperor's Garden at Lahore (1634), consists of two 'char-baghs' and a rectangular terrace

1. Zenana
2. Bath
3. Bedchamber
4. Entrances

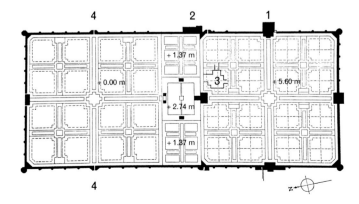

At Lahore, where Shah Jahan resided from time to time, he laid out a second Shalimar Bagh. As in the one in Kashmir, two char-baghs are joined to form a rectangle, separated by a high terrace with a reservoir set crossways. Shah Jahan feared that it might be difficult to maintain the water supply. He therefore did not entrust the design to a landscape gardener but to Ali Mardan, an experienced engineer, who had already achieved fame with his canals and bridges.

The Shalimar Bagh at Lahore is staggeringly similar to the garden of the Taj Mahal (see grey plan, p. 97). If we imagine that the third, uppermost terrace were absent, we would have the structure and proportions of the Taj Mahal garden. The Shalimar Bagh's rectangular marble terrace, accentuated diagonally, tallies with the platform of the Taj Mahal, which is likewise set diagonally to the main axis. A comparison between the two gardens will make clear why Shah Jahan did not wish to place the tomb in the centre of a square garden. A square is oriented upon its centre; and this made it of doubtful appropriateness in several mausolea, since gardens are always situated on a river-bank and have to front the river.

The plan of the Taj Mahal garden could be interpreted differently. Bernier relates that the emperor had planned to build for himself a second structure of the same type, but in black marble, on the other bank of the Jumna, but that the execution of this scheme was forestalled by his imprisonment and deposition. This implies that the garden, as we see it today, was only half of a much grander original design which included the other Taj Mahal and its garden as well as the River Jumna itself, which was to have been spanned by a bridge. Bernier, who compared all Indian gardens and monuments with those in his native land, ends his laudatory remarks about the Taj Mahal with the following story:
'The last time I visited Tage Mahale's mausoleum I was in company of a French merchant, who, as well as myself, thought that this extraordinary fabric could not be sufficiently admired. I did not venture to express my opinion, fearing that my taste might have become corrupted by my long residence in the Indies;

a

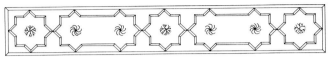

b

Geometric patterns of flower-beds

a) by brick partitions, in the Shalimar Bagh at Lahore
b) by marble partitions, in the garden of the Taj Mahal

and as my companion was come recently from France, it was quite a relief to my mind to hear him say that he had seen nothing in Europe so bold and so majestic[11].'

The Shalimar Bagh and the Taj Mahal garden resemble one another in more than their general layout. Their similarity, which suggests that they were the work of the same architect, is particularly striking in regard to one detail: the division of the flowered borders into star-shaped panels.

The basic form here is a variation on the octagon, consisting of two squares set at an angle to one another, yielding an eight-pointed star. Two of these stars, joined to make a long panel, alternate with simple stellar forms. In the Taj Mahal garden the partitions between them are of marble; at Lahore, on the other hand, brick was considered sufficient. The eight-pointed star is in this case a multifoil design, such as one finds elsewhere only in the ogee arches of contemporary buildings. Circular partitions of this kind could have been constructed of marble only at great cost, but were easily made of brick. Each of the oblong panels features two trees over a carpet of flowers, while the simple stars have only one. One detail alone distinguishes the Taj Mahal garden from that of the Shalimar Bagh: in the former two cypresses alternate with one fruit-tree, whereas in the latter two fruit-trees alternate with one cypress.

In his palace at Shahjahanabad (Delhi) the emperor did not forego the pleasure of spacious gardens either. These covered approximately the same area as the zenana, but were separated from it by the sovereign's private apartments. The two large gardens were called Bakhsh Bagh and Mahtab Bagh ('Life-giving Garden' and 'Moonlight Garden'). The 'Life-giving Garden', like the 'Women's Garden' at Lahore, was evolved from the char-bagh with subsidiary centres in the diagonals and a water pavilion in the middle. The layout recalls that of the Taj Mahal. The scheme of paths and stretches of water concurs in many re-

Feria Bagh, a Mughul waterside palace, equipped with an exemplary system of water supply and sewage

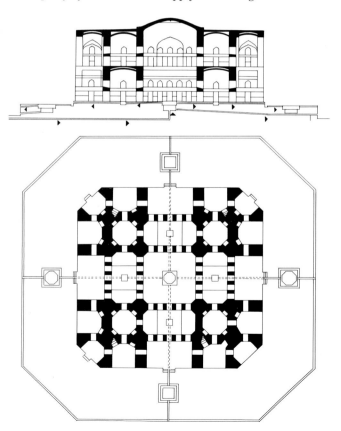

spects with the diagram of the interior of the Taj Mahal (cf. also site plan of the Red Fort at Delhi, p. 138 and of the Taj Mahal, p. 97).

In the Red Fort at Shahjahanabad, next to the 'Life-giving Garden', and separated from it by a high wall, lay the 'Moonlight Garden'. The two constructions differ markedly from one another in layout and in the plants they contain. We may imagine the 'Moonlight Garden' in its original state as a vast complex in which there were only white flowers and black cypresses.

Since in most palaces much of the irrigation system has been destroyed, it is seldom that we are in a position to explain how the channels and conduits were laid out, what the gradient was or in which direction it ran, or how the fountains worked – particularly wherever a channel containing ordinary water fed a fountain from which sprang rose water, or where no conduits are visible yet a fountain splashed away merrily nonetheless. For one seventeenth-century palace, thought to have been built by a viceroy of the Great Mughul, there exists an exact sketch of the building showing all the conduits. Feria Bagh ('Beautiful Garden') is the name given to this waterside palace near Ahmadnagar, which deserves mention on account of its system of pipes.

At Humayun's tomb the water supply could be criticized for not being related more consistently to the concentric layout of the garden. In the Feria Bagh, on the other hand, every conceivable effort was made to repeat the structure of the building in the pipe system. A subterranean conduit carried water from a great distance to the lake surrounding the palace. Beneath the bed of this lake pipes led to the palace, in the centre of which stood a fountain. From the basin constantly filled by this fountain overflow pipes led off in the direction of the four cardinal points, concealed beneath the flooring, and fed smaller basins in the ancillary rooms; from these rooms they ran on to large reservoirs outside the house; the overflow from these reservoirs finally flowed back into the lake.

Plates

The Taj Mahal, Agra

101 The Taj Mahal is situated at a bend of the River Jumna. The mausoleum is here viewed from the opposite bank.

102 The main entrance commands a view over the extensive gardens, since it was raised above the level of the garden. This artifice enhances the spatial effect.

103 Main axis of the garden seen from the roof of the mausoleum. In the background: the entrance gateway.

104 Detail of façade.

105 All four façades of the square tomb are treated in the same way except for the inscribed bands around the main portals.

106 One of the portal niches viewed from below. The transition from the rectangular plan of the niche to its conical upper part presented great difficulties to the geometricians and architects. They chose an abstract twisted cluster of squinch nets, similar to that of the reveals of the arches in I'timad-ud-daula's tomb.

107 The geometric construction of the cluster of squinch nets in the portal niches has not yet been worked out.

108 A detail of a portal niche in the Taj Mahal. Floral designs are encountered on all monuments executed in the late Mughul style.

109 The problem of turning a corner solved in the manner of Persian prototypes. The inlay work consists of innumerable bands of stone.

110 The sepulchral chamber, situated in the centre, viewed from a gallery of the upper storey. In the centre: the cenotaph of Mumtaz Mahal; beside it, that of Shah Jahan.

111 Originally the cenotaph was surrounded by a massive gold wall. While Shah Jahan was still alive it was replaced by perforated marble screens.

112 In contrast to Humayun's tomb, the interior of the Taj Mahal is just as lavishly treated as the façade. The transition to the springing of the dome is effected by squinch nets.

113 On the roof of the mausoleum, above the small rooms at the corners, are marble kiosks. View of the dome of one of the kiosks. In the background: the drum of the main dome.

114 To the west of the tomb stands the tomb mosque; to the east of it, for the sake of symmetry, a similar monument which served as a reception hall during funerary ceremonies.

115 On the roof of the mausoleum.

116 View of the liwan in the tomb mosque. Whereas the mausoleum is faced with white marble that sets off the dark inlay, the tomb mosque is faced with dark red sandstone and the inlay is set off in a light colour. In the interior painted stucco had to suffice.

117 Dome of tomb mosque, viewed from within.

Red Fort, Delhi (Shahjahanabad)

118 Diwan-i-Khas, the Private Audience Hall.

119 Shah Jahan's private apartments, looking along the north–south axis.

120 Perforated monolithic marble screens afford a view out of the Samman Burj over the River Jumna.

121 Interior of the zenana.

122–123 Enclosure walls of the Red Fort.

124 Aurangzib built a small private mosque, the so-called Moti Masjid, within the Red Fort.

125 Interior of the Moti Masjid.

126 Detail of the flat reliefs on the walls of the mosque's court.

127 The court of the Moti Masjid, view to the east.

128 Detail of a support.

Taj Mahal, the tomb of Mumtaz Mahal in Agra,
built 1632–1654
Site plan 1:5000. Elevation, section and ground-plan 1:1000

1 Mausoleum
2 Tomb-mosque
3 Guest quarters
4 River
5 Water tank

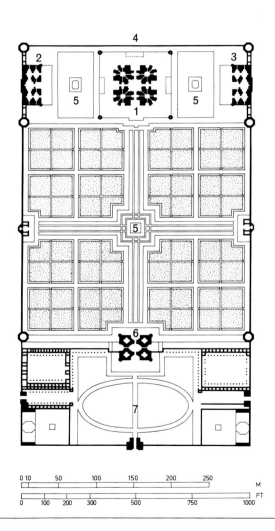

6 Gateway
7 Entrance court
8 Ground floor
9 Upper storey
10 Top storey

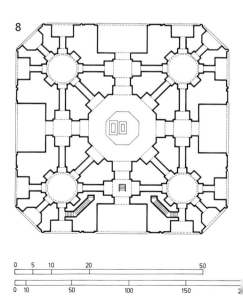

0 10   50   100   150   200   250   M
0   100   200   300   500   750   1000   FT

0   5   10   20   50
0   10   50   100   150

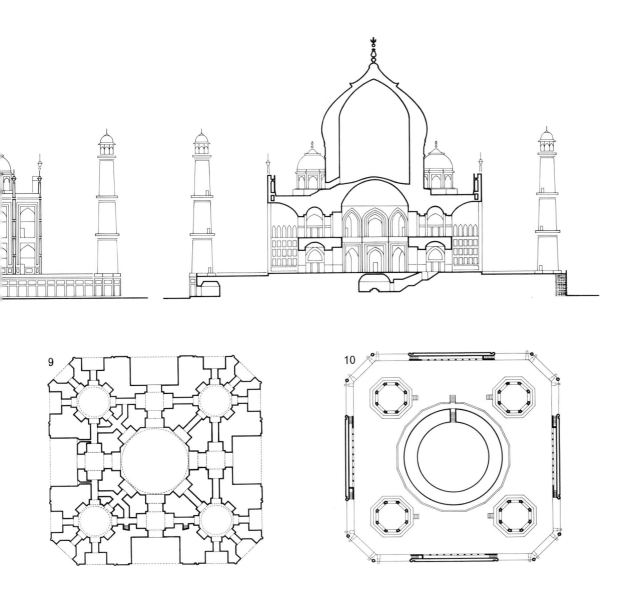

9

10

Notes

Excerpts from a contemporary description of the Taj Mahal

On the occasion of the seventeenth anniversary of the death of Hazrat Mumtaz-uz-Zamani [Mumtaz Mahal] the emperor convened at her shining tomb an illustrious company, distinguished above all by the presence of numerous sage and pious men. Her anniversary was observed and the completion of the mausoleum celebrated. The master of all slaves, the emperor himself, honoured the gathering with his presence. By his prayers and blessing he contributed to the peace of mind of the Chaste One, now at rest in the Gardens of Paradise.

The detailed description of the sacred tomb, submitted to the emperor for his gracious approval, ran as follows: 'The foundations of this monumental building were laid during the fifth year of his reign. The tomb stands on the bank of the River Jumna, which flows past its northern façade. In size and splendour it surpasses even the seven Heavens of Paradise. The foundations were dug as deep as the level of ground water permitted. Skilled artisans covered them with stones set in mortar and made the surface smooth. On this base was erected the platform of the mausoleum, called "kursi", which was unique among those of its kind on account of its height, elegance, decoration and dimensions.

'In the centre of the terrace, upon a platform measuring one "zira" [2 ft. 8 in.] the main body of the building was erected, a paradisaical tomb with a diameter of 70 zira, octagonal in ground-plan in conformity with the octagon–baghdadi. The gleaming dome of the tomb, which spans the main chamber, is worked wholly in marble. Over the inner shell of this dome is another outer one, in the shape of an apple, called "amrud". Its majestic splendour can be appreciated only by an elite of geometricians. The circumference of the dome measures 110 zira; it is crowned by a golden finial 11 zira high, which sparkles like the sun.

'In the centre of the tomb stands the cenotaph, surrounded by a marble balustrade. This octagonal balustrade is made of pierced stone slabs and is most lavishly decorated. The portal is worked in jasper, as are the Turkish chains and belts. The parts of the balustrade are connected by joints worked in gilded iron worth 10,000 rupees.

'At the corners of the platform stand minarets, again supported on plinths, and measuring 7 zira in diameter. These minarets may be compared to a pious man's pleasing prayer ascending to heaven. One also recalls the nobility of the rising star of good fortune or, better still, the knowledge of a sage that he is approaching absolute perfection.

'The most talented artisans have decorated elaborately the entire mausoleum, within and without. The balustrade is covered with many precious stones in various nuances of colour. These were at first artistically polished and inserted by the Panchin Kari [pietra dura] method. All the gems used were of such high quality that even an ocean of descriptions would not suffice to do them justice. Their value cannot be estimated in words.

'By comparison with such beauty the splendour of all eras, the masterpieces of the Arzeng-i-Mani and all the paintings in the galleries of China and Europe are as water, tasteless and not really existent.

'To the east of the mausoleum is a building used for the reception of guests and pilgrims. Apart from a few details it bears a resemblance to the mosque on the west side. The only differences spring from the fact that in a guest-house no mihrab could be let into the rear wall, and that the floors of the halls could not have the form of rows of prayer rugs.'

107

113

I'timad-ud-daula's tomb in Agra, built in 1628
Section, view and ground-plan 1:400

1 View of the ceiling in the mausoleum 1:100

0 1   5   10   15   20 M
0   10   20   50 FT

0   0.5   1   2   5 M
0 1   5   10   15 FT

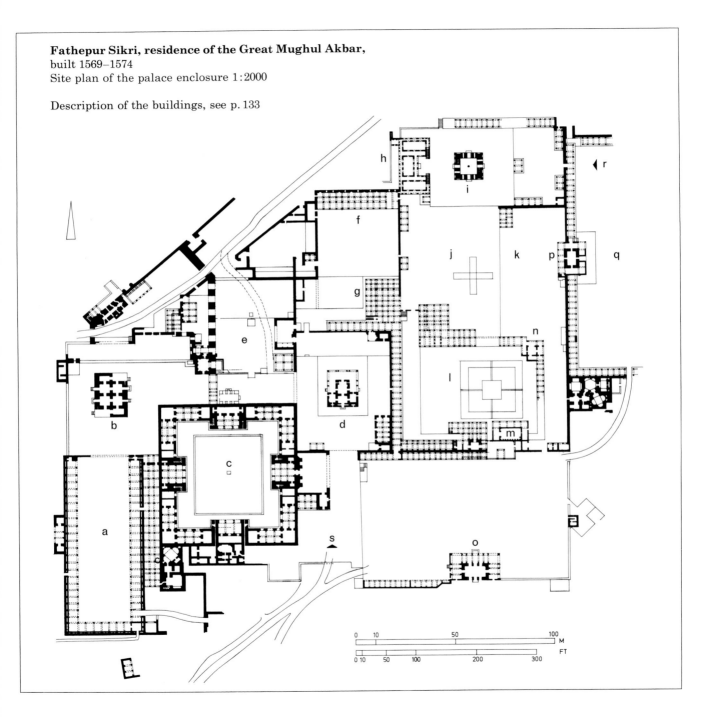

Fathepur Sikri, residence of the Great Mughul Akbar,
built 1569–1574
Site plan of the palace enclosure 1:2000

Description of the buildings, see p. 133

0 10   50   100
M
FT
0 10 50 100   200   300

4. Towns, Forts and Palaces

The towns founded by the rulers of the first Islamic dynasties in India have been destroyed; of most of them only the foundations and enclosure walls have survived. Study of these ruins shows that individual buildings were linked to form small functional groups, but that this was as far as 'town planning' went. In contrast to the builders of cities like Mohenjo-daro and Harappa (2000 B.C.), or to the Hindu sthapatis who right down to modern times designed villages upon a magic grid diagram, Islamic architects frequently left the layout of streets to chance or allowed this to develop organically as the settlement grew in size.

The palace precinct of Fathepur Sikri

It was not until the sixteenth century that one Islamic ruler in India, the Great Mughul Akbar, took on the task of planning an entire residential town, comprising palaces, mosques, caravanserais etc. His old residence of Agra could not be expanded any further owing to the unfavourable terrain, and the emperor grew weary of its noisy and dusty jumble of houses. Frequently he escaped from the cramped palace precinct, with its atmosphere of court intrigue, and took his most crucial decisions in solitude, under the spiritual guidance of a hermit named Salim Chishti, who lived some twenty miles away from the city, on a ridge called Sikri. The country people had many tales to tell about the miracle-working powers of this saintly man; and when he prophesied that a healthy heir would be born to the hitherto childless sovereign at a certain predestined time, the emperor decided to move his residence from Agra to this auspicious mountain, Sikri.

Akbar was extremely tolerant in matters of religion. He favoured neither Muslims or Hindus in his service. It might therefore have been expected that when he built his new residence he would revert to the ancient Indian tradition of town planning and commission a Hindu architect to design his new residence of Fathepur Sikri ('town of victory, Sikri') in accordance with the precepts of the 'shilpa shastras', which at that time were still common knowledge. But the emperor evidently disapproved of such

131

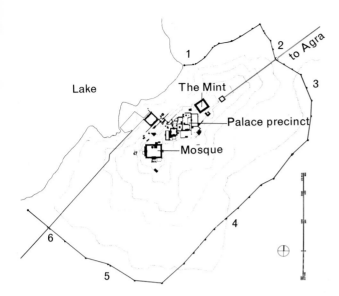

Plan of Fathepur Sikri, the residence founded by Akbar in the 16th century. Only the palaces, mosques and parts of the town wall have survived.

1. Delhi Gate	3. Birbal Gate	5. Tehra Gate
2. Agra Gate	4. Gwalior Gate	6. Ajmer Gate

town plans with their suggestive symbolism, rooted in the Hindu concept of the cosmos. He preferred to live in a town which had no such metaphysical scheme but had a layout adapted to the natural features of the terrain.

The rectangular town wall was thus laid out with its longer sides running parallel to the line of the ridge; along its axis, i.e. from north-east to south-west, ran the principal thoroughfare, which led to the highest part of the ridge where the palace stood. Only on three sides was the rectangular town enclosed by a wall; to the north-east it fronted on a lake, formed artificially in some low-lying ground by damming a river. Today the lake has dried up and the houses of the townsfolk on either side of the ridge have disappeared, for – in contrast to the palaces and mosques – these were built of perishable materials such as clay, wood and straw. The many buildings

erected in more durable red sandstone afford us a clear picture of the original design. This was never effaced by any later additions or renovations, as was the case with other Mughul residences at Agra, Delhi and Lahore; for shortage of water compelled the emperor and his suite to leave these buildings after they had been occupied for less than two decades.

Construction of the first palaces began in 1569, and in 1572 one of the finest houses, that of Raja Birbal, and the Great Mosque were completed. Already in 1585 the town's water requirements could hardly be met from the artificial lake; and as the local well water was polluted Akbar gave orders for the court to move to Lahore. None of his descendants ever resided in this, the finest and most magnificent of all Indian capitals.

In 1585 William Finch, the English traveller, saw the town shortly before it fell into decline. In his account of his travels he relates:
'From thence [Agra] we went for Fatepore [Fathepur Sikri], which is the place where the king kept his court. The towne is greater then Agra, but the houses and streetes be not so faire. Here dwell many people, both Moores and Gentiles... Agra and Fatepore are two very great cities, either of them much greater then London and very populous. Betweene Agra and Fatepore are 12 miles, and all the way is a market of victuals and other things, as full as though a man were still in a towne, and so many people as if a man were in a market[12].'

The Foundation of Fathepur Sikri

Our plan shows that not all the buildings fit in with the general orientation of the town. The caravanserais, mint, treasury and baths, located on the hillside, follow the natural contours, i.e. the axis of the town, whereas the mosque had to be oriented toward the cardinal points so that the mihrab might point toward Mecca. In so far as the plateau on top of the hill made it possible, this orientation, which no doubt was regarded as luckier, was also adopted for private apartments and courts. But since the plateau extends from the south-west to the north-east, and the ideal orientation ran from north to south, the different courts had to be staggered one behind the other.

Near the mint, in the north-east of the city, the main road from Agra leads into the Court of Public

Palace precinct at Fathepur Sikri, viewed from above

a) Stables for camels and horses
b) House of Raja Birbal
c) Jodh Bai palace
d) Miriam's garden
e) Miriam's house
f) Hospital and garden
g) Panch Mahal
h) Emperor's study
i) Diwan-i-Khas, the Private Audience Hall
j) 'Pachisi' court
k) Garden
l) Emperor's private apartments
m) Emperor's sleeping quarters
n) House of the Turkish Sultana
o) Administration and archives
p) Diwan-i-'Am, Public Audience Hall
q) Court of Public Audiences
r) Entrance
s) Entrance reserved for imperial family

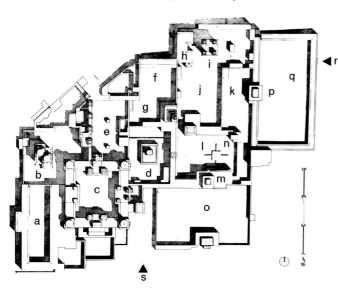

Audience, or Diwan-i-'Am. Every citizen was granted admission to this court when the king was receiving petitions or pronouncing judgment. The raised throne-pavilion of the emperor is set in an axis of the court; the entrance to the court is not located on this axis, so that it was impossible for the emperor's subjects to draw near to him directly; instead they had to approach the throne from one side, in an attitude of humility. This is reminiscent of the ancient Oriental custom whereby one did not enter a house or a court directly but by an entrance set at an angle. Let us recall in this connection the swastika-shaped entrances to Vedic villages or the circumambulatory path around the stupa (cf. 'India', in this series). Even the 'Pearl Mosque' built by Aurangzib in the private precincts of his palace at Delhi kept to this traditional form of entrance, which is rooted in Vedic symbolism but also makes the house more defensible.

From the Diwan-i-'Am, by way of an insignificant-looking door, access is gained to the court with the Hall of Private Audience, or Diwan-i-Khas. On entering this court the visitor finds, in the axis of the door by which he entered, a small reception pavilion; behind the two-storeyed hall in which the audiences were held, along the same axis, are the royal offices. Characteristically, here too, in spite of the axial layout of the different buildings, it is not possible for the visitor to approach the audience hall axially, whereas the sovereign, entering from his study, could stride directly into the hall from a westerly direction. Thus a symmetrical and axial arrangement was evidently used only where it had real symbolic value.

Whereas some visitors were permitted to enter the Hall of Private Audience, the emperor assembled in an adjoining 'game court' only a few invited guests for a game of 'pachisi' or some other form of amusement. In the south an arcade separated the pachisi court from the private apartments of the emperor. Here, too, every kind of symmetry was avoided. The sleeping and living quarters were flush with the walls of the court; covered passages, formerly closed off by stone grilles, led in various directions to the rooms of Akbar's favourite wives.

The town plan differs from earlier Hindu plans in that there are no streets anywhere in the entire palace precinct, and only very few rooms have walls on all sides. Open spaces, enclosed by walls but staggered and adapted to differences of elevation, are the basic elements in the architecture of Fathepur Sikri. Presumably the walls of the court were erected first, and then the individual buildings, verandahs and colonnades, arranged along the wall as necessity dictated, as though they were moveable fittings. At any time it was possible to add an extra pavilion or to erect a hall of prefabricated pillars, architraves and latticework; all elements are of the local red sandstone. Small pavilions, measuring no more than two, three or four axial units are not, as one might think, relics of longer arcades: such pavilions were simply erected anywhere along the wall of the court as the need arose. A movable plan such as this recalls the tent cities of Akbar's ancestors. Even today at festival time in India one finds such groups of gaily coloured square pavilions, whose form is based on that of tents. During the monsoon they give protection against the rain and during the hot season against the sun, but at the same time allow the cool winds of evening to waft pleasantly through them. We may imagine the stone 'tent halls' of Fathepur Sikri as surrounded by an equal number of real tents, made of fabric and decorated with rugs. It is even conceivable that the game court, for example, was from time to time covered over completely.

The joins in the pavement of the courtyard show that pachisi, an ancient Indian game, was played here instead of on a board as was usual. Tradition has it that the game was played with slave girls wearing garments of different colours instead of with the customary wooden figures. Abu-'l-Fazl, the court historian, relates:
'At times more than two hundred persons participated in this game and no one was allowed to go home until he had played sixteen rounds. This could take up to three months. If one of the players lost his patience and became restless, he was made to drink a cupful of wine. Seen superficially, this appears to be just a game. But His Majesty pursues higher objectives.

He weighs up the talents of his people and teaches them to be affable.'

It can no longer be ascertained with certainty what purpose many of these buildings served. On the west side of the pachisi court there stands, for example, a five-storeyed structure known as the Panch Mahal, which lends a particular emphasis to the silhouette of the palace. It has five halls with pillars, one above the other; each is of smaller dimensions than the one below, so that the whole edifice forms a tiered pyramid based on the multi-storeyed wooden monasteries during the era of Hinayana Buddhism. But the stone pyramid at Fathepur Sikri differs from its prototypes by its asymmetrical structure. It is a further example of the reservations which the architect – or the ruler – felt about the axial quality of Hindu buildings, rooted as this was in Hindu cosmology (see grey plan, p. 37).

In their materials and mode of construction all these buildings are purely Hindu, i.e. indigenous.
The forms of building, on the other hand, do not conform at all to the Hindu ideal of massiveness in architecture. The playful free composition of the palace courts could be regarded almost as a kind of protest against traditional Indian architecture, closely controlled as it was by the priests; it was as a result of this tradition that the style of Hindu temples became petrified, already before the Muslim invasion, into a meaningless monumentality. A comparison suggests itself here with the development of European architecture in the nineteenth and twentieth centuries. In both cases men broke away from a monumentality devoid of content and from such conventional notions as 'street' and 'square', in order to attain forms that were freely adapted to their function and environment. When walking through these courts, situated at various levels, one has the sensation of being transported into some utopian city of the future.

The particular charm of Fathepur Sikri lies in the fact that the underlying idea of the town plan was not implemented ad absurdum, but at a few focal points gave way to an appropriate monumentality.

This is best illustrated by the Private Audience Hall, a two-storeyed masonry building (see grey plan, p. 38). Its actual form is of no interest, since the façades are ill-proportioned and the Hindu 'panch-ratna' system, which is suggested by the four kiosks on the roof, lacks the dominating central dome. But the interior, with its rich symbolism, is among the most original creations of Indian architecture. In the centre of the two-storeyed chamber stands a monolithic column, with a projecting ring of consoles to support the platform that bears the imperial throne. There is an unmistakable allusion here to the ancient Indian myth according to which the ruler of the universe reigns from its axis. Also the walkways which lead from the throne diagonally across the chamber are obviously symbolic allusions to the Hindu concept of the cosmos (see p. 24/25).

Several contemporaries of Akbar note that the so-called Ibadad Khanah ('Hall of Worship') at Fathepur Sikri was completed in 1574. It was to this building that the emperor invited the sages of the land for theological disputations.

It may be assumed that the four-winged auditorium so described is the audience hall known as the Diwan-i-Khas. The diagonal walkways do indeed divide the hall into four parts, oriented toward the cardinal points. No other chamber that has been preserved in the palace fits this vague description.

The earliest building in the town seems to be the Jodh Bai palace. A spacious walled square, windowless on the outside, encloses this symmetrical complex. This palace is a typical 'atrium house'; it is neither a body of masonry like the Diwan-i-Khas, nor a building with pillar halls freely arranged along one wall of the court. Its four quarters form a symmetrical structure consisting of self-contained apartments. The entrance to the court is set axially, but in this case too it is not in line but to one side, so that one cannot see into the court from outside. A small guardhouse in front of the gateway indicates that this palace was built as a fortified building, which stood isolated amid the surrounding countryside, already before the adjoining courtyards were designed.

On the west side of the palace, north of the stables built for the horses and camels, the system of enclosed courts leads to a spacious platform. This is not walled but offers an unrestricted view of the lake and the gardens in the north-western part of the town. On this terrace, which is underpinned by vaulting, stands the so-called house of Raja Birbal (see grey plan, p. 57/58). Like the audience hall Diwan-i-Khas, it is a detached structure of masonry and represents an exception among the buildings of the court. Whereas most of the colonnades extend from the enclosure walls into the open court, the house of Raja Birbal is a structure of interior chambers enclosed on all sides and related to a central axis.

The ground-plan is one of classical simplicity. The lower storey consists of a suite of four chambers which are exact cubes, as well as two entrance porches which project forwards from the building. In the upper storey two squares of the ground-plan, i.e. the north-eastern and south-western squares, are built upon, forming domed cubic chambers. In front of each of these two rooms is a square terrace, one of which is shady in the afternoon and the other one shady in the morning (see p. 28).

The domes above the upper storey and the saddle roofs above the entrance porches on the ground floor are double structures; this serves to prevent the rooms becoming too hot in summer – a precaution quite essential in a tropical climate, particularly where the rooms are closed. The principle of insulation by double walling is also to be met with in Akbar's offices. Hooks fixed on either side of a double row of columns were used to affix carpets in lieu of walls, in two layers if need be. These afforded protection against the cold of the Northern Indian winter as well as the summer heat, and also kept the offices and conference halls free of noise.

The house of Raja Birbal is built exclusively of stone. But by sculptural embellishment of the walls a wooden Hindu pillar structure could be simulated down to the last detail. The delicately worked facing in red sandstone reproduces lattice-work architecture with lavishly ornamented fillings. The dome, too, was built in imitation of wooden prototypes. Whereas the simulated lattice-work supports have no static function to fulfil but serve a purely decorative purpose, the ribbed domes adopt not only the shape but also the construction of Hindu wooden domes. (For the origin and development of the ribbed dome, see Chapter 5.)

At Fathepur Sikri Islamic types of arches appear alongside Hindu pillars, consoles and architraves. The soffit of the Islamic ogee arch would be decorated with a Hindu motif, the foliated garland; at the same time Hindu pillars and brackets would be Islamized by two-dimensional geometric carving (see p. 31).

Is it possible that one and the same architect could have designed buildings such as the house of Raja Birbal and the Diwan-i-Khas, a house built around a court like the palace of Jodh Bai and the colonnades of the pachisi court? Is not the manner of treatment of these buildings fundamentally different? The 'movement' of buildings rotating around an axis is different from that of buildings scattered freely around a court. A viewer standing in a court is himself the centre of all the architecture, which appears to move around him. This relationship is reversed if a viewer moves around a massive masonry building, the centre of which is inaccessible to him. He can walk around the buildings – he will feel as though they are rotating upon their own axis – but always remain an 'outsider', so to speak, even when entering the rooms in the interior. It is not the observer who constitutes the point of reference, but the axis of the masonry. This is why in the Diwan-i-Khas the axis runs only half-way up the height of the room as a column, and is then continued to the ruler's throne.

Even before Akbar moved his court to Fathepur Sikri, he began to build the fort of Agra over the ruins of an earlier citadel. Its massive masonry, lined with red sandstone and crowned with battlements, has the shape of a sickle whose curve faces to the west.

The eastern side of the fort lies on the bank of the Jumna. Most of the palaces have been destroyed, and it is only in the south-east that some complexes have survived in toto. The Jahangiri Mahal (see grey plan, p. 77) is the most important monument to have been preserved – apart from the 'Pearl Mosque', which was not built until the reign of Shah Jahan. Although it was named after Jahangir, Akbar's son, this palace no doubt originates already from the reign of Akbar.

Stylistically the Jahangiri Mahal is related to the house of Raja Birbal, but in its ground-plan it differs greatly from all its prototypes at Fathepur Sikri. We can attempt to explain the heterogeneity of Akbar's dwelling quarters only by supposing that, due to the Islamic tributary system, architects from the most diverse parts of Asia congregated at the court of the Great Mughul, who readily appreciated their exceedingly varied notions.

In contrast to the palaces at Fathepur Sikri, with the exception of the Jodh Bai palace, the Jahangiri Mahal is markedly symmetrical in plan. Like the general layout of the fort, it is closed off on the west side and has a terrace fronting on to the river in the east. Analysis of the ground-plan leads to the following conclusions. The asymmetrical alignment of the northern parts of the building was apparently not envisaged in the original design, which provided that the palace should terminate in a symmetrical fashion, as in our attempted reconstruction (a).

In the ground-plan we can follow an interesting interpenetration of Persian and ancient Indian ideas of how to treat space. Fig. (b), a reconstruction of the ground-plan, shows that it was divided into a 'Persian' and an 'Indian' group of rooms. In the east we can make out an unfinished Indian palace in which all the courts and rooms are grouped in annular form around the large central court, which is suggestive of square Hindu diagrams (see 'India', in this series); the other three parts, however, exhibit a variety of architectural forms and associations. In the niches of the portal, which open on to Court II, we can detect the Persian prototype already in the

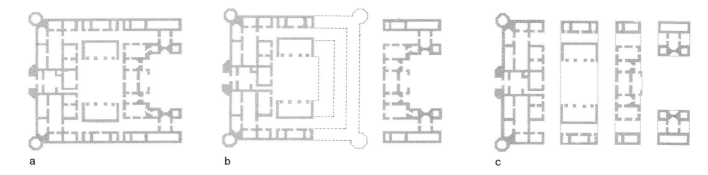

a

b

c

Jahangiri Mahal in the Red Fort at Agra

a) reconstruction of the original plan
b) reconstructed ground-plan, showing division into an
   ancient Indian and a Persian sequence of rooms
c) division into an entrance zone, reception rooms, library
   and zenana

ground-plan; the elevation (see grey plan, p. 77) makes
the difference even plainer. Court II is surrounded
by Persian façades with ogee arches, and Court I by
Indian façades with pillars, widely projecting brackets, architraves and 'chayas' (see p. 62).

The main axes of the palace intersect in the large
square Court I. In contrast to the open spaces at
Fathepur Sikri, this court forms the centre of a
sequence of rooms. In view of its modest proportions,
and those of the façades fronting on to it, one is
inclined almost to regard it as nothing less than the
main chamber of the palace. It is closed off to the
east and west by an almost unbroken area of wall,
whereas to the north and south it adjoins two large
reception halls. If we consider these three rooms as
the most important sequence, we may conclude that
the ground-plan is divided into three main zones. If
we also take into account that the corner buildings
in the north-east and south-east open on to the cons-
tricted circular courts through niches in the portal
– i.e. are contrasted with the rest of the building by
the fact that all the façades are treated in the same
way – then the ground-plan is divided according to
Fig. (c): an entrance zone comprising the servant

quarters; the ruler's apartments; the library and
offices; and finally two square pavilions which we
may take to be zenanas, as they are exposed to cooling
breezes.

In the entrance zone, as in all palaces erected
during Akbar's reign, we find evidence of this contrast between Persian axial buildings and Hindu

Reception hall in the palace of Man Singh, in the fort at
Gwalior, 15th century

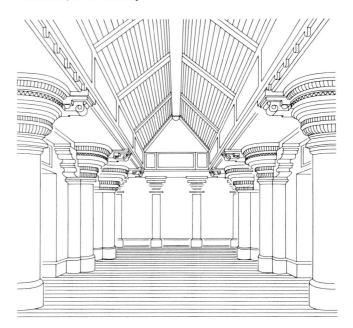

tradition. The architects' ideal was that one gate should follow upon another and one room upon another. However, the man who commissioned the building thought that the entrance should be staggered, which was not compatible with axiality.

A comparison between one late Hindu palace and the Jahangiri Mahal will illustrate the transition from Hindu to Islamic forms of secular building.

The fifteenth-century palace of Man Singh in the fortress at Gwalior shows that Hindu palace architecture, as well as that of temples, was in a state of decline. Eclectic movements and 'excessive configuration' without reference to any strict formal canon are characteristic of this decadent phase of Hindu architecture. It is difficult to estimate what blessings flowed from the restrictions which Islamic rulers imposed upon their Hindu craftsmen. The plane, which in Islamic art acquired the same importance as the mass enjoyed in Hindu art, placed a limit upon all formal exuberance. Top-heavy columns such as those in the Man Singh palace, which are decorated eclectically and flout all the canons of statics, are transformed in the Jahangiri Mahal into massive rectangular pillars overlaid with a finely spun veil of Islamic geometric compositions. Curved chayas are reduced to their original form of simple eaves; sinuous consoles are corseted into a rectangular grid, and their sloping faces resolved into flights of steps. Without this reductive process, from which no sultanate in the whole subcontinent could escape, the decline of Indian architecture would inexorably have continued. Hindu temples built after the spread of Islam across Asia testify to this decline.

The Red Fort of Delhi

Each of the great Mughul forts – Agra, Lahore and Delhi – offers us today only an inadequate impression of the original layout, since the British pulled down a large part of the buildings to make way for new barracks.

Even Akbar wearied of his residence at Agra and

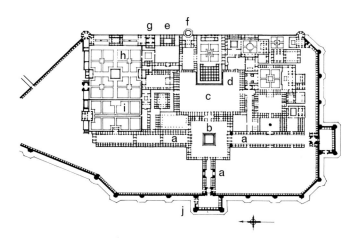

Red Fort at Delhi, built for Shah Jahan

a) Bazaar
b) Naubat Khana, Music Pavilion
c) Public Audience Court
d) Diwan-i-'Am, Public Audience Hall
e) Diwan-i-Khas, Private Audience Hall
f) Samman Burj
g) Bath
h) Bakhsh Bagh, 'Life-giving Garden'
i) Mahtab Bagh, 'Moonlight Garden'
j) Entrance

moved to Sikri, as we have seen; Shah Jahan, too, shortly after acceding to the throne, began to look for suitable terrain on which to build a new residence. Bernier, a French physician at the court, relates that the town was not suited as the residence of the emperor since in summer it was intolerably hot. It was impossible to return to the ruins of the old towns at Delhi, since they were too cramped. Fathepur Sikri was also out of the question, since there was no way of remedying the water shortage. The court astrologers, who although Hindus exerted a considerable influence, thought they had found auspicious terrain on the west bank of the Jumna, to the north of the towns of Old Delhi. They advised that the foundation stone be laid on Friday, 9th Mahavam 1048 A.H. (1638 A.D.), for on this day the constellation of the stars would be most favourable. The construction of the town of Shahjahanabad (Delhi), with its so-called

'Red Fort', lasted for nine years without interruption. The power of the Great Mughuls had reached its zenith; material and labour from all parts of India and neighbouring countries were at the emperor's disposal. When he entered the city, accompanied by his suite, nine years after work began, marble monuments sparkled with inlaid precious stones and courts were laid with costly carpets; the ruler himself wore priceless jewellery, and during the long procession had pieces of gold showered upon him by his son.

Original plan of Red Fort at Delhi (utilization plan)

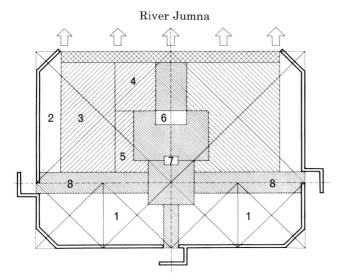

░░	Mardana
▨	Emperor's private apartments
▨	Semi-public areas
▨	Zenana

1. Soldiers' and attendants' quarters
2. Princes' apartments
3. Gardens
4. Private Audience Hall
5. Administration
6. Public Audience Hall
7. Music Pavilion
8. Bazaars

River Jumna

For what seems to us today the paltry sum of 10,000,000 rupees (equivalent to $1,000,000 or £417,000), the architects Hamid and Ahmad had built for the emperor a residence of which the fame was swiftly to spread beyond the borders of the Oriental empires to the courts of European monarchs.

In what ways may the Red Fort be distinguished from the palace at Fathepur Sikri? Do they have any features in common?

Shah Jahan was an orthodox Muslim. Unlike Akbar, he did not sympathize with other religions, and correspondingly did not allow his architects to choose between different spatial concepts. During Akbar's reign architecture was as flexible as the sovereign's outlook on the world; Shah Jahan's architecture was as simple as his orthodox beliefs. The site plan of the Red Fort is characterized by emphasis on the axial relationship between successive courts, whereas at Fathepur Sikri a relationship of this kind, as we know, did not exist.

The Red Fort at Delhi was evidently planned as a rectangle with sides in the proportion 3:4; in the east it fronts on the River Jumna, but since an arm of the river would have formed an acute angle with the north wall, the architect preferred to include this triangular area within the walls of the fort. Only for this reason does the wall have an irregular shape and fail to conform to the almost rectangular plan of the palace. The southern corners of the rectangle formed by the walls are cut off; corresponding recesses in the north-western and north-eastern corners may be explained by the fact that the architect had a symmetrical plan in mind.

The palace was divided by its east-west axis into a northern and a southern part, in the proportion 1:1. The visitor enters the fort along this main axis, on which lie the reception courts. Perpendicular to this it was planned to build a long bazaar, extending from the south gate to another one in the north; this bazaar divides the palace in the proportion 1:2. Since the north wall lay along the river-bank, there could be no north gate and the bazaar from the start lacked the connection it needed with one of the streets of the town. The northern part of the bazaar thus formed a blind alley; whether it was ever completed or used is open to doubt.

The original 'utilization plan' looked as follows. One-third of the area of the fort, i.e. the area west of the large bazaar, was reserved for the servants' and soldiers' quarters. Whoever entered the palace had at first to traverse this zone through a long passage. At the point where the north-south and east-west axes intersect there is a square court, still accessible to the public. By way of the 'naubat khana', or music gatehouse, from which musicians announced the arrival of the emperor or other prominent dignitaries, one reached the court of public audiences.

In the eastern periphery of the fort, on the east-west axis, lie the emperor's private apartments, which form a second axis running from north to south; without exception they are oriented toward the Jumna – recalling a similar alignment in the fort at Agra. Between the northern part of the bazaar and the imperial chambers there were gardens and offices; to the north of the gardens lay the houses of princes. South of the east-west axis lay the zenana area.

The architectural features of the palace at Delhi bear a considerable resemblance to those of the palace at Fathepur Sikri: predominant in both cases are pillared halls abutting the walls of the court; nevertheless the strict disposition at Delhi produces a more impressive total effect. Each courtyard is co-ordinated with other areas by its axes, which form a cross. Asymmetrical tower-buildings like the Panch Mahal on the pachisi court at Fathepur Sikri would be inconceivable here. Architecture had become the mirror image of an entrenched monarchical system.

The different possibilities of the climate

At Fathepur Sikri, Agra and Delhi people lived mainly in the open air. If the emperor expected to find the climate more pleasant in his new residence at Shahjahanabad, he was destined to be disappointed. In summer the heat in this city is more intense than it is at Agra. It was hardly possible to spend much time in rooms enclosed by walls on all sides. Marble halls open on all sides and subdivided here and there by monolithic lattices were regarded by the Mughuls as the type of building best suited to the climate. Only the baths form an exception. These were cooled by chill water in summer; in winter, when hanging carpets provided an imperfect insulation for the other rooms in the palace, they could be heated.

A watercourse passes through all the halls on the east side. On account of its cooling effect it was called the Nahr-i-Bihisht, or 'Stream of Paradise'. This canal was fed, as was the extensive water supply system of the whole fort, from a sluice at the north-east corner of the enclosure wall. This was the terminal point of an aqueduct which began 50 miles upstream near Khizrabad. Even in the summer months it provided the palace with fresh water from the upper reaches of the Jumna. Already during the reign of Firuz Shah work had begun on this conduit, but it had to be interrupted. Shah Jahan commissioned the engineer Ali Mardan to complete it. Only after he had tried out different routes did he in fact succeed in bringing the water all the way to Delhi.

Bernier, who was granted admission into the zenana quarters only once, during the emperor's absence, relates:
'Almost each room has a separate basin with running water near the door. Everywhere one encounters gardens, fine avenues, shady bowers, rivulets, fountains, grottoes and other low-lying places which afford protection against the sun, as well as airy halls and terraces suited for sleeping in at night.'

The enclosure walls of the fort and all the courtyards and bazaars as far as the Diwan-i-Am, the Public Audience Hall, were all built of red sandstone or at least encased in this material. The private apartments, on the other hand, were executed throughout in white marble. Their intarsia of precious stones, gleaming marble lattices, ceilings decorated in gold and silver, silk curtains to provide shade, and Persian carpets created a fabulous atmosphere like that of the 'One Thousand and One Nights', which led European visitors to send home enthusiastic accounts.

The architecture of the Great Mughuls' court was emulated in many residences of provincial governors

A garden pavilion in the Kotilal (fortress) of Delhi built in the 14th century is kept cool by large masses of earth and masonry

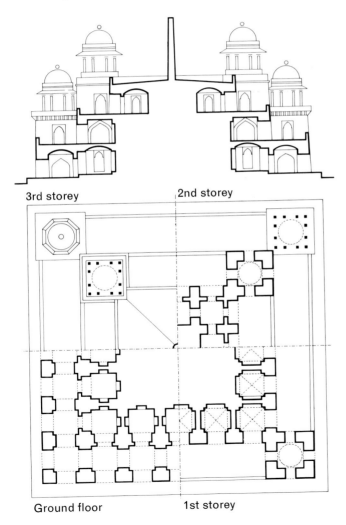

3rd storey   2nd storey

Ground floor   1st storey

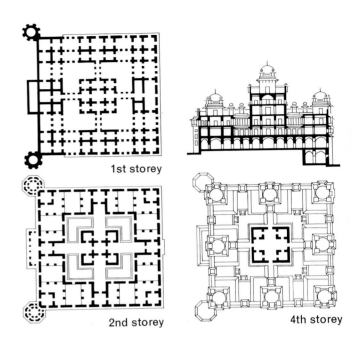

1st storey

2nd storey   4th storey

At Datiya, at the height of the Mughul style, a Hindu prince built a palace which conforms to ancient Hindu architectural concepts

and independent Hindu rajas. Engrailed arches, filigree stone lattices and other elements of Mughul architecture may be encountered in all parts of the empire, even in the modest houses of townspeople. Nevertheless the form of some small residences in Northern India shows that they did not all emulate unreservedly the prototypes of Agra, Fathepur Sikri, Lahore and Delhi. This may partly be due to the fact that the influence of Hindu architects and artisan guilds was greater the further one went from the imperial court. But the decisive factor was probably that the Islamic rulers and their Hindu subjects entertained different conceptions of the ideal type of dwelling. The ancestors of the Great Mughuls were nomads who preferred the open spaces of the Central Asian steppes to a settled abode. Modelled upon nomadic tent cities and influenced by the grandiose courtyards of Persian caravanserais, the Mughuls built their palaces in the form of rows of interconnecting courts. They cooled them with running water and air, for the slightest breeze could pass unhindered through these pillared halls.

Another possible way of keeping the rooms cool had been tried out and brought to perfection by the Hindus many centuries earlier. They insulated small interior rooms by enclosing them within extremely thick walls; occasionally these were even built underground.

The open halls of imperial palaces were exposed to the hot winds, which were particularly unpleasant when accompanied by sandstorms. Even large stretches of water nearby and several rings of fountains did not cool the air sufficiently. For this reason Firuz Shah had built a pavilion modelled on the Hindu type, the so-called Kotilal (fort) at Delhi, which, in contrast to the later airy pavilions of the Mughuls, is a massive stepped building, like a stepped pyramid, with small chambers in the interior. The Kotilal in Old Delhi and the Datiya palace in the Bundelkhand district, built by the Hindu prince Bir Sing Deva, are derived from the monolithic copies of Buddhist terraced buildings that stood on the sea shore at Mahaballipuram and are today known as 'rathas' or 'celestial chariots' (see 'India', in this series). In its structure and details the Datiya is the most Hindu palace of Hindustan. What an irony of history it is that it should have been built as late as the flourishing period of the late Mughul style!

Also in regard to the function which its rooms fulfilled the Datiya bears a resemblance to the Kotilal. Some important rooms were evidently subterranean. The accesses are blocked up; but several contemporary accounts tally in suggesting that the rooms and halls of the palace also continued below ground. The same sequence of rooms as was built of ashlar masonry above ground level was dug out of the rock as a sequence of caves, and contained just as many storeys. In a palace of this kind the ruler could choose the rooms with the most suitable temperature.

Geometric compositions

According to Islamic teaching it was forbidden to represent human beings and animals.

Strictly geometric ornament appears in Islamic architecture during the tenth century. The earliest examples include small lattices in the al-Hakim mosque in Cairo, the segmentation of which is derived from the star of David. Also in the monuments of the first sultans in Delhi we encounter simple geometric compositions. The use of these was, however, limited to small window apertures pierced through the stone, called 'jalis'. The wall faces of Iltutmish's tomb or that of Alai Darwaza are indeed decked with characters, zigzag bands, festoons etc., but do not yet have geometric designs which could be combined to form an infinite network.

Early Arab inroads into the plain of the Punjab during the eighth century and the foundation of a small Arab state around the town of Multan led to the introduction into India of two-dimensional designs. As an example, we may mention the brick façade of the twelfth-century tomb of Yusuf Gardizi.

Stone lattices divided geometrically are to be found in many Northern Indian mosques dating from the thirteenth, fourteenth and fifteenth centuries; but as a rule these are small and the draughtsmanship is simple. The flourishing period of geometric ornament in India began with the rule of the Great Mughuls.

With the return of Humayun from Persian exile, Persian artisans arrived in Delhi. In Humayun's tomb we meet for the first time jalis taller than a man, perforated according to a geometric plan – so much so that no more than a pattern of thin fillets remains. Monolithic lattices of this kind were carefully finished wherever they could be examined closely, whereas inaccessible windows in the drum of the dome were worked less carefully.

Similar structures, such as lattice-screen windows built up from the basic forms, the square and the

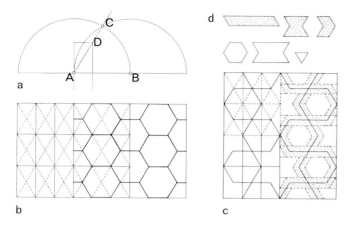

Fig. I
a) construction of a triangle with angles of 60°
b) a row of triangles with 60° angles makes possible a hexagonal pattern
c) method of transferring a hexagonal pattern on to the dome of Humayun's tomb
d) the white and red stones used

point where these two circles intersect yielded an equilateral triangle. Each rectangle upon the baseline AB whose diagonally opposed corners A and D lie upon the side of the triangle AC is suitable as the basis of a design consisting of hexagons and six-pointed stars. The simplest kind of lattice of this type, a series of hexagons, is seldom used. A great favourite, on the other hand, was the alternation between a hexagon and a six-pointed star, such as we find both in Humayun's tomb and in that of I'timad-ud-daula (Fig. I/c). The joints in the mosaic on the drum of Humayun's tomb show distinctly that, in order to rationalize the work, an effort was made to use as few elements as possible: three white and three red pieces sufficed (Fig. I/d). Since these could be made to interlock, they could be cut from long bands of stone without chipping too much of the material away.

Octagonal compositions

Wherever square panels had to be filled, hexagonal designs could not be used, since with them care had to be taken that the corner points of the basic unit had the form occurring in the centre of the basic unit. Only when this condition was fulfilled could the design be repeated serially.

In the simple octagonal pattern (Fig. II/b) octagons

Fig. II
a) and b) method of designing a simple octagonal pattern
c) pattern produced by superposing one octagonal design upon another, e.g. in the paved paths in the Taj Mahal garden

octagon, recur on the floor of Humayun's tomb in mosaic worked in white marble and red sandstone, but in this case they alternate with the hexagon and the star of David. The drum of the dome, which in Persia is frequently tiled, was here likewise encased in a stone mosaic. Its geometric structure is also evolved from the star of David. We shall begin our analysis of various geometric compositions with this simple example.

Hexagonal compositions

If, from any design based on a hexagon, we take a single segment – the basic particle which, when repeated, produces the whole figure – we shall find that it invariably consists of a number of rectangles in a very precise proportion to one another. This rectangle has diagonals at angles of 60° and 30° to the sides (Fig. I). The artisan constructed these proportions in the following way. He drew a semicircle of any radius and then from the centre of its baseline (B) drew a second semicircle with the same radius. The lines connecting the centres of these two circles with the

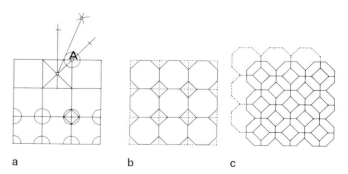

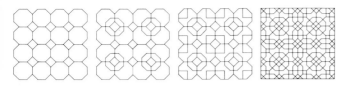

Fig. III
Method of designing an intricate octagonal pattern, e.g. in the large screen-walls at Fathepur Sikri

are placed side by side, and the interspaces form small squares. The lattice is constructed as follows: in Fig. II/a the angle formed by a diagonal and an axis of a square is bisected. A circle drawn around the corner point (A), to which the line bisecting the angle forms a tangent, is the circumscribed circle of the small square desired.

The paths in the Taj Mahal garden were covered with stone slabs arranged in an octagonal pattern; as a variant to the simple octagonal pattern it was overlaid by a second one, the position of which was adjusted until the central points of the octagons in the former pattern coincided with the centres of the squares in the latter one (Fig. II/c).

In the case of monolithic lattice-screen windows more intricate designs were chosen. During the reign

Fig. IV
Method of designing an octagonal pattern that occurs in the tombs of Salim Chishti and I'timad-ud-daula

of Akbar the following composition was frequently used at Agra (Fig. III). The basic structure was a simple octagonal pattern. This was overlaid by another pattern of the same type, the position of which was adjusted in the same way as in the last example. However, of each nine octagons in the second pattern only the four in the corners were actually executed; the one in the middle was replaced by a square, the sides of which had the same length as the width of the octagon. This composition was brought to completion by combining the axes of all the small squares to form a third pattern by drawing a few connecting lines.

Scarcely any Mughul building lacks another octagonal composition, carried out as inlay work, as mosaic or as a monolithic lattice-screen window. In its centre is an octagon of which the inner connecting lines form an eight-pointed star, the latter having the shape of two squares turned at an angle to one another (Fig. IV). The finest execution of this pattern may be seen on the plinth of I'timad-ud-daula's tomb at Agra. The lines of the pattern were left as white marble fillets, while the panels were filled in with coloured stones. The work was done in successive stages, as follows:

Stage 1: a simple octagonal pattern was drawn and these octagons were separated from one another by erasing two of the four sides of the squares between them.

Stage 2: an eight-pointed star was drawn into these octagons, as shown in Fig. IV/2.

Stage 3: on each two sides of this eight-pointed star

1 2 3 4 5 6

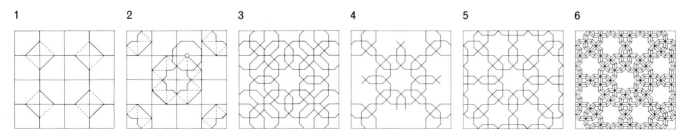

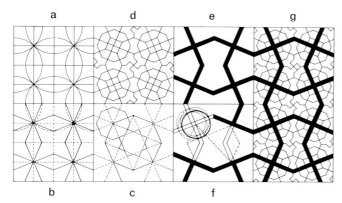

Fig. V
Sometimes, as here in I'timad-ud-daula's tomb, a more delicate 'secondary' composition was added to the rougher 'primary' one

a small octagon was fitted in, as shown in Fig. IV/3, the centre of each small octagon lying on a corner of the large octagon.

Stage 4: two sides are erased from each small octagon.

Stage 5: the small open octagons are connected by a few lines with the adjacent octagon, which is likewise an open one.

Stage 6: each line of the pattern is replaced by a band measuring the width of the marble fillet (in a mosaic), or by the rods of the lattice, which are prismatic in cross-section (in a jali window).

The sculptors of the Islamic countries devised increasingly intricate combinations of forms. In order to avoid the monotony which results from a simple variation of hexagons and octagons, or a superposition of one upon the other, they began in Akbar's reign to give the lattice pattern a rhythmic effect by making the stellar forms more compact and by widening the interspaces between the stars. The climax of this development is the marble lattice in Salim Chishti's tomb.

In search of means whereby these forms could be refined still further, artisans hit upon the idea of interpolating in a primary composition – which might be either a combination of star of David and hexagon or an octagonal pattern – a secondary composition of finer and more delicate workmanship. Geometric patterns of this kind have two planes, irrespective of whether they are viewed from within or without, the fillets of the secondary composition being worked until they are thinner than the primary one. As an example we may consider a perforated marble screen on I'timad-ud-daula's tomb (Fig. V). Its primary composition is derived from a pattern of squares. In filling in the remainder planes of this primary pattern with a secondary composition (Fig. V/e), the artisan did not proceed from the central lines of the broad marble fillets but from the border of each dovetail-shaped panel (Fig. V/f). In order to ensure that the measurements of all forms were correctly proportioned in relation to this change, the borders of the panels were completed to form a new octagon, so obtaining the new measurements of the so-called small octagons and the squares which they contained. This artifice leads to no formal problems of any kind, since all the lines of the secondary composition run into one another as they did previously, although

Fig. VI
Method of designing a dodecagonal stellar pattern

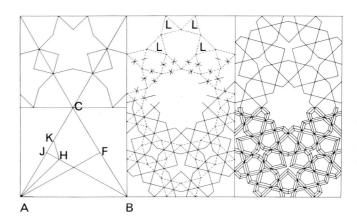

145

new central points have been obtained on the other side of each marble fillet. The objective of preventing the lines from becoming too dense near the broad fillets has thus been achieved (Fig. V/g).

Dodecagonal compositions

Like sexagonal compositions, dodecagonal (twelve-sided) ones can also be seriated only if they are designed within a rectangle of which the angle between the diagonal and the sides measures either 60° or 30°. Once again care must be taken to ensure that one quarter of each form drawn in the middle of the figure recurs in the corners. The construction of the dodecagonal design depicted here begins as follows. The basic composition consists of a central dodecagon, which is linked by squares to the segments of dodecagons in the corners. The length of the sides of the squares and of the dodecagon is equal. This prerequisite is fulfilled if the radius of the dodecagon is determined in the following way. In the triangle formed by joining points A, B and C, two perpendicular bisectors are drawn. The line bisecting the angle FAJ meets the other perpendicular bisector at H. From this point a half-right-angled turn (45°) is made, to reach the side AC. The distance between the point K thus obtained and point C yields the diameter required. Now the corners of the dodecagon which are not contiguous with the square are combined with the corners of the nearest square. Thereby triangles are formed (L). In these triangles one inscribes further equilateral triangles, and the sides of these are protracted as follows:
a) in the squares to the point where the lines protracted from the circumjacent triangles meet and form a four-pointed star;
b) in the dodecagons to the point where two protracted sides of the triangle meet on one of the twelve radii;
c) in the remaining irregular hexagons to the point where two protracted sides of the triangle meet on a bisector. (Fig. VI.)

Within the framework of this brief survey we do not seek, nor would it be at all feasible, to give a

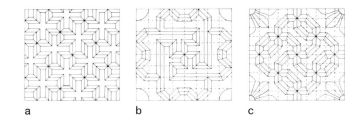

a   b   c

Fig. VII
In the sandstone panels of the House of Raja Birbal Hindu artisans endeavoured to incorporate the swastika symbol into geometric patterns

representative cross-section of the innumerable geometric compositions that are to be met with in Indo-Islamic monuments. Compositions with ten, eleven, sixteen and eighteen corners were just as popular as the simpler examples discussed above. Some heavily Hinduized compositions may still be mentioned, although these are far less subtle in design. Only in India were attempts made to give a symbolic significance to the Islamic play on geometric forms, by introducing the ancient Aryan solar symbol of the swastika. Several arrangements of this kind are to be found in the fillings of walls and ceilings in the house of Raja Birbal at Fathepur Sikri.

It is particularly tempting to set the swastikas in a row with their corners touching one another. This yields cruciform remainder planes whose juxtaposition produces a relatively stable equilibrium (Fig. VII/a). Of greater interest is the combination of swastika and octagon; but for this many connecting fillets are required, some of which terminate on transversal lines in a quite amateurish way (Fig. VII/b). Only once was the attempt made to use the swastika in a classical geometric composition by turning its arms into an octagon (Fig. VII/c). The Hindu artisans' lack of practice in designing such compositions means that even in this case the result cannot rival basic schemes adopted from Persia.

Plates

Mosque at Gulbarga

151 On the roof of the mosque, looking west toward Mecca. This mosque is the only one in India to have a court covered by domes.

152 In the arcade wide arches support the barrel roofs, built crosswise.

153 In the court area the small domes are supported by a dense network of narrow arches.

154 Detail of the arcade.

155 Diagonal view of the ground floor.

Gol Gumbaz, Bijapur

156 The Gol Gumbaz, viewed from the roof of a gateway to the south.

157 The tomb of Sultan Muhammad 'Adil Shah is approached through an unfinished gateway.

158 The tomb, the third largest domed chamber in the world, remained unfinished; the faces of the walls were likewise unworked.

159 The sepulchral chamber narrows at the level of the springing of the dome as the arches interpenetrate, forming a circular gallery. Here, the vast round dome viewed from this gallery.

160 In the ground floor of the gateway the Archaeological Survey of India renovated some panels of the ceiling, which show various uses of the cluster of squinch nets.

161 The squinch net evolved in Persia by superposing several ogee arches one upon another. The artisans at Bijapur were obviously unfamiliar with the geometric derivation of this design; they executed a network of twisted quadrilaterals which do not follow any geometric principle.

Yantar Mantar at Jaipur

162 The so-called 'rashis' in the observatory at Jaipur made it possible to study the motion of the stars at certain moments in the ecliptical system. The incline of each instrument points exactly to the pole of the ecliptic; the semicircle is parallel to the earth's orbit.

163 One of the rashis.

164 A rashi viewed frontally.

165 Segment parallel to the earth's plane at the Equator, viewed from the measuring scale of a yantra lying parallel to the earth's axis. Steps were built on either side of the marble measuring scale so that readings could be made from close up.

166 In the centre: a movable brass measuring instrument which served as a model for yantras and rashis.

167 Inside a circular implement a vertical steel rod casts its shadow on to a horizontal segmented circle. By this means the sun's azimuth and altitude can be ascertained. Passages were left between the areas where measurements were taken.

168 In the foreground: a rashi. In the centre: two hemispheres, accessible from below ground level, from which it was possible to take measurements on the equatorial system.

169 Between the autumn and spring equinox a pin parallel to the earth's axis casts its shadow on to the surface of this sundial, which is turned towards the South Pole. A second circular area for taking readings during the six summer months is on the back of the same instrument.

170 View from inside one of the two hemispheres, accessible from below ground. These were built of white marble and red sandstone by the Maharaja Jai Singh for taking measurements on the equatorial system.

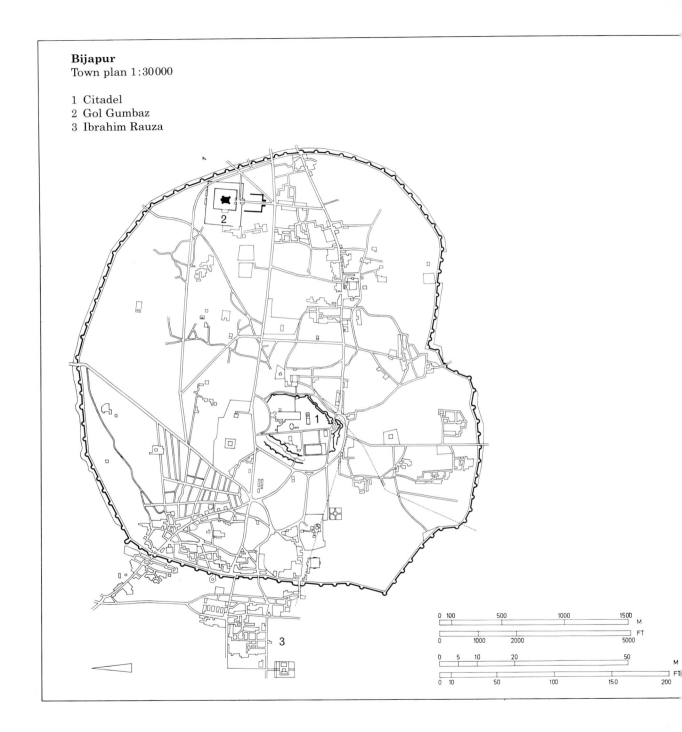

Bijapur
Town plan 1:30000

1 Citadel
2 Gol Gumbaz
3 Ibrahim Rauza

2

1

3

0 100   500   1000   1500
                              M
                              FT
0   1000   2000   5000

0 5 10   20   50
                              M
                              FT
0 10   50   100   150   200

Gol Gumbaz, Sultan Mohammed 'Adil Shah's tomb,
built 1626–1656
Section, view and ground-plan 1:1000

1 Ground-plan of the vault's floor
M Inner foundations
N Outer foundations

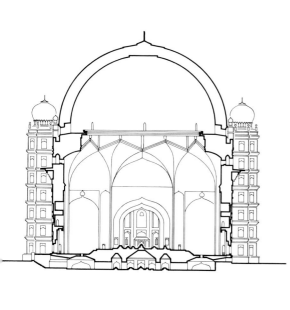

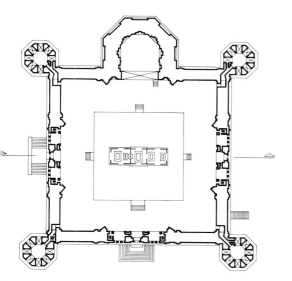

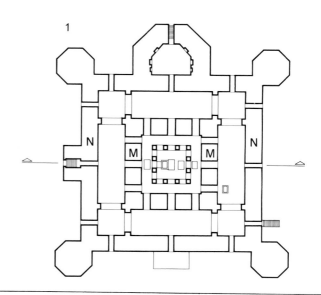

Notes

Yantar Mantar at Jaipur

During the eighteenth century, when the empire of the Great Mughuls was already weakened and the centres of art and architecture moved to the residences of independent Hindu princes and provincial governors, the wealthy ruler of the principality of Amber, Maharaja Jai Singh II, implemented a unique architectural concept.

His intense interest in astronomy soon led him to realize the limitations set by ordinary brass instruments upon accurate measurement of the course of the stars. Telescopes were still unknown; thus stellar measurement of any kind had to be made by visual sightings with the aid of mechanical instruments. The sun could be measured with the aid of a sundial.

The Maharaja envisaged two possible improvements: (1) by enlarging the instruments one hundred times he hoped to obtain measurements one hundred times as accurate; (2) by building stationary instruments he hoped to avoid the inaccuracies which resulted from the use of metal instruments with adjustable axes and other movable parts. For this reason he built in the cities of Delhi, Mathura, Benares, Ujjain and Jaipur exceptionally large towers with sloping walls and circular marble dials. Particularly splendid were the buildings laid out in one court of his palace at Jaipur. The bizarre sundials, marble hemispheres accessible from below ground level and other strange constructions are not just instruments but also, on account of their size, buildings in their own right with interior chambers, steps, doors and occasionally even windows.

The wall faces, gleaming in red, yellow or white, only seldom bear the ornaments characteristic of the late Mughul style. The monumental effect of the entire complex derives from the geometrically determined, bold plastic quality of all the masses of masonry.

The crude subdivision of Indian architecture into a Hindu and an Indo-Islamic phase does not do justice to this kind of building. Yantar Mantar, with its functional structures serving technological purposes, is not related to any stylistic trend. Nevertheless its forms are not solely functional. Some ruler or architect of genius may have had the idea of creating, here in the heart of India, a configuration of abstract spaces which anticipates and surpasses all the endeavours of our twentieth-century Cubists.

A Mughul court architect, if faced with the same task, would probably have enclosed such dials and measuring lines within buildings of a conventional Indo-Islamic type. Maharaja Jai Singh II, on the other hand, realized the new possibilities of treatment made possible if the strict forms employed for purposes of measurement were transferred to all the remaining parts of the building as well. Each mass of masonry in the observatory is subject to the same geometric canons as are the planes and lines used in measurement of the stars.

Do not the observatories of Northern India testify to one of those epochal moments in the history of architecture, when men abandoned outmoded spatial ideas and formal canons, which had survived only for tradition's sake, and set out afresh, free from all axioms other than those set by the task in hand?

Jai Singh's achievement baffles us today primarily because these bold forms look like a creation of the twentieth century, and moreover are far less well known and thoroughly studied than all other endeavours by early architects in the direction of Cubism. The grandeur of its conception can be assessed properly only if, instead of comparing Yantar Mantar with modern works, we judge it in its contemporary context: if we bear in mind that Hindu architecture had by the fourteenth century already become petrified into an expressionless monumentality, and that in late Mughul buildings the decadent forms and proportions represented an eclectic blend of influences from Europe and the Orient.

169

The Jami' Masjid in Gulbarga, built 1367
Section and ground-plan 1:500

1 Components of the construction
2 Sketch of the system

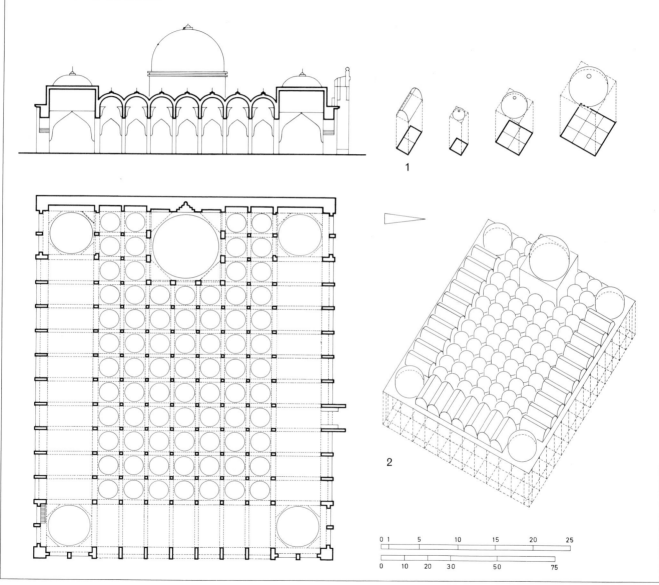

1

2

0 1   5   10   15   20   25

0   10   20   30   50   75

Comparative size of various buildings 1:1000

1 Pantheon, Rome
2 Gol Gumbaz, Bijapur
3 Taj Mahal, Agra
4 Diwan-i-Khas, Fathepur Sikri
5 Panch Mahal
6 House of the Raja Birbal, Fathepur Sikri
7 Tomb of I'timad-ud-daula, Agra

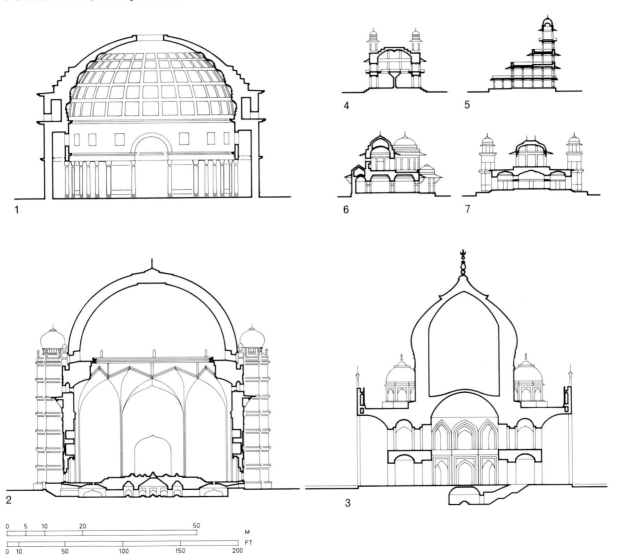

172

5. Material and Construction

Building costs

Abu-'l Fazl, Akbar's court historian, endeavoured in his chronicle 'Ain-i-Akbari' to provide as full an account as possible of life at court, the nobility, the level of knowledge, the pursuits of the emperor – in short, to cover everything he thought worth handing down to later generations.

He did not even omit to mention the thirty most popular recipes, giving the exact amount of salt, ginger or melted butter to be used in cooking the most important and tastiest dishes.

Akbar's personality appeals to us today not so much on account of his original philosophical views, or his love of hunting and good company, or even his statesmanship, but rather on account of his work as a builder. Abu-'l Fazl overlooked the importance which a planned town like Fathepur Sikri has in the history of architecture. His chronicle does, to be sure, have a chapter 'On Building', in which we learn the prices of the materials used, the wages of the labourers employed, and the specific gravity of all the kinds of timber known; but this contains no reference to the design, the manner of execution, or the person of the architect. Regrettable as this may be, we must nevertheless be grateful for the facts we are given, which do at least throw light upon the economic aspects of the work:
'Regulations for house-building in general are necessary; they are required for the comfort of the army, and are a source of splendour for the government. People that are attached to the world will collect in towns, without which there would be no progress. Hence His Majesty plans splendid edifices, and dresses the work of his mind and heart in the garment of stone and clay. Thus mighty fortresses have been raised, which protect the timid, frighten the rebellious, and please the obedient. Delightful villas, and imposing towers have been built. They afford excellent protection against cold and rain, provide for the comforts of the princesses of the Harem, and are conducive to that dignity which is so necessary for worldly power.

'Everywhere also "sarais" have been built, which are the comfort of travellers and the asylum of poor strangers. Many tanks and wells are being dug for the benefit of men and the improvement of the soil. Schools and places of worship are being founded, and the triumphal arch of knowledge is newly adorned.

'His Majesty has enquired into every detail connected with this department, which is so difficult to be managed, and requires such large sums. He has passed new regulations, kindled the lamp of honesty and put a stock of practical knowledge into the hands of simple and inexperienced men.

'Many people are desirous of building houses; but honesty and conscientiousness are rare, especially among traders. His Majesty has carefully inquired into their profits and losses, and has fixed the prices of articles in such a way, that both parties are satisfied[13].'

We may now give some extracts from Abu-'l Fazl's explanatory comments on the most common building materials of his age. As currency units he mentions 'rupees' or 'dams'; 40 dams equal 1 rupee. (Ten rupees are approximately one modern U.S. dollar.) The most common unit of length is the 'gaz'. The exact length of one gaz has been fixed by Dr Chaghtai at 0.79 metres. (This calculation was made possible only by the discovery of a manuscript in which the measurements of the Taj Mahal are given in gaz.) One gaz equals 24 'tassuj'.

The unit of weight is the 'ser'. Forty sers equal 1 'man' (approx. 13½ kilograms) or 14 'tolas'. (Certain numerals are referred to by names: thus for 100,000 the Hindus say 1 'lakh', and for 10 million use 1 'crore'.)

Red sandstone [writes Abu-'l Fazl] costs 3 d[ams] per man. It is obtainable in the hills of the Fatehpur Sikri, His Majesty's residence and may be broken from the rocks at any length or breadth. Clever workmen chisel it so skilfully, as no turner could do with wood. Pieces of red sandstone, broken from the rocks in any shape, are sold by the p'hari which means a heap of such stones, without admixture of earth, 3 gaz long, 2½ g. broad, and 1 g. high. Such a heap contains 172 mans, and has a value of 250 d.

Bricks are of three kinds: burnt, half burnt, unburnt. Although the first kind are generally made very heavy, they weigh in the average three sers and cost 30 d. per mille. The second class cost 24 d. and the third 10 d. per thousand.

Tiles. They are one hand long and ten fingers broad, are burnt, and are used for the roofs of houses, as a protection against heat and cold. Plain ones, 86 d. per mille; enamelled, 30 d. for ten.

K'has is the sweet-smelling root of a kind of grass, which grows along the banks of rivers. During summer, they make screens of it, which are placed before the door and sprinkled with water. This renders the air cool and perfumed. Price, 1½ R. per man.

Silver clay is a white and greasy clay, 1 d. per man. It is used for whitewashing houses. It keeps a house cool and looks well.

Glass is used for windows; price 1 R. for 1¼ s., or one pane for 4 d.

Iron door-knockers, from Persia and Turan, tinned; large ones, 8 d. per pair; small ones 4 d. Indian door-knockers, tinned, 5½ d.; plain ones, 4 d.

Screws and nuts, chiefly used for doors and boxes. Tinned, 12 d. per ser; plain, 4 d.[14]

The wages of the poor artisans were lower even than those of foot-soldiers. A bricklayer received approximately 2 rupees a month and a woodworker only 1¼ rupees per month, whereas ordinary soldiers earned between 2½ and 10 rupees. For the sake of comparison we may quote some other salaries that are also mentioned in the 'Ain-i-Akbari'. The commander of ten infantrymen drew 7 rupees, ordinary female attendants in the harem up to 20 rupees. The salary of members of the imperial harem was between 1,000 and 1,600 rupees.

From the wages of the artisans and the costs of the materials we can calculate the cost of building certain palaces. But we do not know the actual cost of any single monument built by Akbar.

On the other hand, for Shah Jahan's Red Fort at Shahjahanabad (Delhi) the total costs are given in a chronicle from the reign of Aurangzib. Its compiler, Bakhtawar Khan, gives the following figures (in lakhs of rupees):

Wall and moat	21
Bazaars and workshops	4
Emperor's apartments	28
Diwan-i-Khas, including silver-plated ceiling and furnishings	14
Rang Mahal, including bedroom and garden	5½
Diwan-i-'Am (Public Audience Hall)	2
Hayat Bakhsh garden and Hamman (baths)	2
Palace of Begum Sahiba and other ladies	7

Including additional expenses the cost of the Red Fort amounted to about 100 lakhs, or 10,000,000 rupees. This is much less than the emperor spent on the tomb of his favourite consort at Agra. The total cost of the Taj Mahal was 185 lakhs, i.e. 18,500,000 rupees, of which 5,000,000 went on building the actual tomb and the rest on the auxiliary buildings and garden.

For more than a thousand years it was customary in India for rulers not to finance the building of a temple, mosque or tomb out of their personal fortune. Thus, during the eleventh century, many villages and towns in the Chola empire were made liable for the building and maintenance of the great temple at Tanjore; similarly, during Shah Jahan's reign, thirty villages near Akbarabad (Agra) were obliged to pay for the construction of the Taj Mahal out of their annual revenue of 40 lakhs of rupees and the taxes which they collected from nearby shops and caravanserais.

The manuscript in which Ustad Isa is mentioned as the architect of the Taj Mahal has been identified by Dr Chaghtai as a forgery from a later period. Besides the name of the architect it contains a list of names, birthplaces and wages of the leading artisans. Although the value of these data has been challenged, we may quote this list here.

A bricklayer from Kandahar named Muhammad Hanif received a monthly wage of 1,000 rupees. He was assisted by Muhammad Sayyid from Multan, who had a salary of 590 rupees and by Abu Torah, also from Multan, who earned 500 rupees. From Constantinople there came a specialist in dome construction, Isma'il Khan Rumi, whose salary was 500 rupees. The experts in constructing the crowns of domes were Muhammad Sharif from Samarkand and Qasim Khan from Lahore; they received 500 and 295 rupees respectively per month. The inscriptions were the work of Qwadr Zaman, whose salary was 800 rupees. The 'pietra dura' work was designed by Chiranji Lal from Kanauj for 800 rupees; his assistants, likewise Hindus from Kanauj, were Chotilal, Mannu Lal, and Manuhar Singh, who earned between 200 and 380 rupees. The designs of the floral patterns were the work of 'Ata Muhammad and Shaker Muhammad, both from Bokhara, whose salaries ranged between 400 and 500 rupees. The architect responsible for the landscaping, Ram Lal Kashmiri by name, came from Kashmir. We also hear of Amanat Khan, a master of inscriptions from Shiraz, whose salary was 1,000 rupees; he is the only artist of whose actual existence we can be certain, for his name also occurs on an inscription in the interior of the mausoleum.

Construction of the dome

Already prior to the Muslim invasion domes were constructed to roof dwellings and temples. The Hindus distinguished between two methods of construction which developed organically from the various materials used in building. The so-called 'ribbed dome' – a framework of bamboo canes tied together at the vertex – was derived from the earliest Indian method of construction in bamboo. By adding a horizontal framework a dome was obtained, of which the silhouette took on the shape of a circular or ogee arch.

The 'corbelled dome' developed from Megalithic structures consisting of piled-up stone blocks or slabs. It is built up out of rings of horizontal courses and is usually conical in outline. Corbelled domes, also called 'false domes', can be identified in many early cultures. Even in historical times Indian artisans were unwilling to abandon this construction, which the Hindu priests preferred for theological reasons.

From the eleventh century onwards, after the Muslim invasions, new types and constructions found their way to India. In addition to the straight architrave there appeared the Islamic pointed arch, which in India always took the shape of an ogee arch. Besides the Hindu types of dome mentioned above there appeared the so-called 'true dome', whose joins point towards the centre of the hemisphere.

All three types of construction can be traced in Indo-Islamic architecture up to the era of the Great Mughuls.

Ribbed domes

The earliest specimens of ribbed dome that have survived are to be encountered in the apses of Buddhist chaitya-halls.

The large dome in the centre of the Jami'Masjid at Champanir is constructed according to prototypes of this kind. As in the Jain temples on Mount Abu (Gujarat) and in many other Indian temples, eight architraves resting on pillars form the base of the round dome. Sixteen curved ribs comprise the structural framework, the interspaces between the ribs (squinch nets) being filled in with stone slabs.

The same construction was also employed for the smaller domes of the Jami'Masjid at Fathepur Sikri. In both cases the inserted stone slabs are apparently held in position by small attached fillets, which make

The ribbed stone dome in the mosque at Fathepur Sikri was built by the same method as had been employed in ancient Indian wooden buildings

the ribs look T-shaped in cross-section. Like many such details, the shape of these ties, without which a construction of this kind would collapse, has not yet been adequately explained.

In the Jami'Masjid at Fathepur Sikri a ring of stone – the same light-coloured limestone as was used for the ribs – is to be seen at the springing of the dome. All the other structural members and the fillings between the ribs are of local red sandstone. By contrasting the colours it may have been intended to accentuate the static ribbing. The stone ring at the springing of the dome may serve as a tie securing the lower ends of the ribs. Naturally a ring of this kind could not be made from a single piece of stone. The ribs, too, each consist of three parts. It can be established with certainty that the individual stones of which it was made up were held together by cramps.

Corbelled domes

In almost every Indian temple we encounter the corbelled dome, built up of projecting courses. Above a building with a square ground-plan it appears in

176

the form of a pyramid; often the square is reduced to an octagonal shape by architraves set diagonally across the corners, and the circular courses begin over this octagonal base. This produces a dome in the shape of a truncated cone. All the smaller domes of the Jami'Masjid at Champanir are constructed from corbelled courses – a clear indication that Hindu artisans alone were employed on this building. Hindu architects usually made the outer silhouette of a corbelled dome approximate to that of a stepped pyramid. Islamic builders, to whom the symbolism of a Hindu stepped monument was alien, presumably insisted that a dome should be round, like those they knew from their homelands. For this reason mortar was piled on in large quantities until the outer silhouette of the truncated cone took on a rounded form.

Examples of this kind of dome are plentiful in Northern India where the corbelled dome was used to roof small and large pavilions and tombs, particularly under the sultans of Delhi.

An almost sensational example of a corbelled dome is the Gol Gumbaz at Bijapur. In the relevant literature it is generally overlooked that the third largest dome in the world is built upon a Megalithic principle! However, the individual bricks, set in horizontal courses, are embedded in so much mortar that the dome might be called one of mortar to which bricks have been added.

The largest pure corbelled dome in India forms a vaulting over the Hindu temple of Surya at Konarak; in the nineteenth century it was found to be on the verge of collapse and was therefore completely underpinned. In the Gol Gumbaz, too, cracks were discovered a few years ago, but the dome could be saved by affixing to the inside a shell of reinforced concrete some 12 centimetres thick.

It is hardly possible to analyse the statics of the Gol Gumbaz since the building's stability is determined by a variety of factors. Normally a horizontal thrust occurs in a corbelled dome which has to be absorbed in the horizontal joints through frictional resistance unless each course is secured by ties. This rule does not apply to the Gol Gumbaz since a cast bowl – and this is what the dome could be called – is self-supporting and only exerts vertical pressure upon the masonry below.

In ensuring the stability of a conventional domical structure it is of the utmost importance that there should be heavy vertical stresses to receive the horizontal thrust of the dome. The lighter the vertical stress and the greater the horizontal thrust, the further the resultant of all the forces is shifted to the periphery, so endangering the stability of the building. For this reason architects of large domical structures seek to place vast masses of masonry at the springing of the dome.

Some historians of architecture take the view that the masonry of the Gol Gumbaz is for this reason strongly reinforced below the dome with intersecting arches, arranged in a way that we have yet to discuss. This yields a broad gallery above the masses of masonry that have been shifted towards the interior.

If a hemispherical dome like that of Gol Gumbaz does indeed serve only to transmit vertical stresses to the masonry, this precautionary measure is superfluous. In all probability the architects at Bijapur did not yet think in terms of static systems of this kind. In their experience a dome consisting predominantly of mortar was relatively stable; but steps were also necessary to prevent it collapsing when cracks appeared on the bowl and pressure was exerted outwards – as the future was to show.

Special kinds of construction
Cast ceilings

If the cast dome of the Gol Gumbaz deserves to be called a corbelled dome on account of its horizontally set bricks, most of the vaultings at Bijapur are pure cast forms which are not liable to collapse even when most of the underpinning has been destroyed. Many kinds of ceiling which at first glance seem puzzling

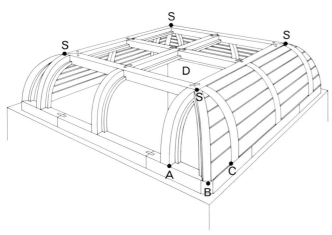

Cutaway diagram of a coved ceiling from the Mughul period

were made possible by the use of mortar, which is extremely stable. Thus for example the survival of the flat ceiling over the sepulchral chamber of the Ibrahim Rauza, which has a span of about 33 feet, can be explained only in the following way: the thin intersecting stone beams and the coffered panels between them do not, as one might expect, form the ceiling but are merely the mould for the supporting layer of mortar.

Coved ceilings

In Akbar's palaces we encounter – as well as domes, vaulting and flat ceilings – coved ceilings, a prominent feature whose structure, like that of the ribbed dome, was adopted from ancient Indian wooden buildings. These coved ceilings may be constructed over square or rectangular rooms. The stone framework was erected with the aid of stone ribs (either unipartite or bipartite, depending on the size of the room) and without centring; the panels in this framework were then filled in with stone slabs. The framework is stable if no distortion of the terminal stone ribs on top of the walls is liable to occur. This is easily prevented if these stone ribs are not only secured in the masonry but are also bound together by iron cramps.

In the first stage of construction the curved stone ribs A, B and C were erected, which we can regard as the flexibly mounted trusses that made up the framework. Each pair of them formed a triangle that was proof against distortion; all three together formed a pyramid, the apex of which (S) was immovable. In the second stage the four S points were braced by horizontal beams, which were reinforced by extra beams (D) if the span was very wide.

Coved ceilings of this kind are to be found in the Diwan-i-Khas at Fathepur Sikri and the southern reception hall in the Jahangiri Mahal at Agra.

Bengali roofs

In Shah Jahan's palaces and Aurangzib's 'Pearl Mosque' we encounter a special type of barrel-vaulted roof which was introduced to the capital cities of the Great Mughuls by Bengali artisans.

Out of the bamboo construction from which almost all types of Indian building can be derived there evolved in Bengal, with its rainy climate, a type of roof which gave the impression that all its planes were curved. The ridge and the eaves were upturned; also

The arched vaulting of the so-called 'Bengali roof' is derived from ancient Indian bamboo structures

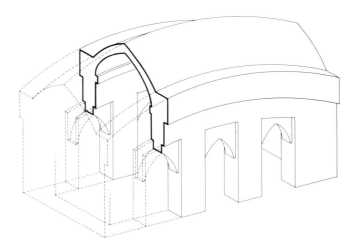

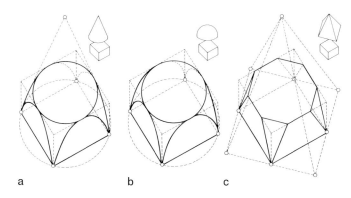

a   b   c

Three methods commonly used in Asia to effect the transition from a cubic space to the circular springing of a dome

a) spherical pendentive (Santa Sophia), formed by intersecting the cube with a sphere
b) conical pendentive (Egypt), formed by intersecting the cube with a cone
c) 'Turkish triangle', formed by intersecting the cube with a pyramid

the bamboo rafters placed perpendicularly to the ridge were curved.

This type of roof was translated into wood and stone before the Muslim invasion. Since it was Hindu architects who built the mosques of their Islamic conquerors, most Bengali mosques have barrel-vaulting with ogee arches.

Squinches, 'Turkish triangle', pendentives, stalactites and interspaces between ribs (squinch nets)

In the Mediterranean lands the construction of domes was only possible over small areas until architects had devised a suitable transition between the ground-plan, which was usually square, and the circular springing of the dome. The most ingenious solution of this problem, which involved both the form and the stability of the building, was to be found in Santa Sophia in Constantinople, built in the sixth century A.D. This achievement of Byzantine archi-

tects deserves particular emphasis since there were only incomplete prototypes for the transitional plane used in Santa Sophia: the spherical pendentive.

The spherical pendentive is an interspace formed by intersecting a hemisphere with a cube. Although equally satisfactory in terms of both stability and form, it was confined to the Mediterranean area and Asia Minor. Nor did a variant of this, the conical pendentive – an interspace formed by intersecting a cone with a cube – find its way either into Persian or into Indian architecture. It is still hard to explain why Persian architects did not follow the prototype of Santa Sophia but instead sought more intricate transitional planes and forms independently. A lack of knowledge of Byzantine architecture cannot be the reason for this, since there was intensive commercial contact between east and west, which led to an exchange of experienced craftsmen.

In Persia the structure of domes developed without being influenced by western prototypes, which proved to be of great importance in the evolution of Indian domes.

The Persian architect proceeded from the fact that by changing a square ground-plan into an octagon the dome could rest upon eight points, so that the different shapes of the octagon and circle would not

a) In early Persian design the wall surfaces between the squinches were geometrically ill-defined
b) If a squinch were placed in a wall surface laid across a corner, it looked unsightly when viewed from below

a
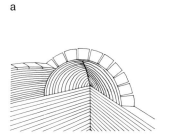

b
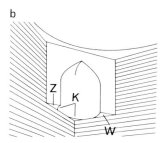

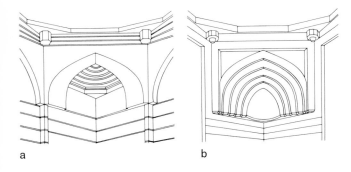

a   b

Indian solutions of the squinch problem:

a) Iltutmish's tomb, Delhi (1236)
b) Jamaat Khana, Delhi (1320)

present any problems as regards stability. Instead of stone architraves, which he did not have at his disposal, he chose the round arch, built of brick, to span the corners of the square. The backing of these round arches – almost conical planes with an arris, which starts in the corner and ends in the round arch – has a form known as 'Persian squinch' (a). The Persian architect shifted the position of the walls in such a way that one end flowed into the circular springing of the dome and the other flowed into the round arch of the squinch. This interspace is not well defined geometrically. In his search for greater clarity of form the architect decided to place the round or pointed arch in a wall face set diagonally across the corner (b). In this way he could avoid boldly curving interspaces between squinches. However, this solution led to fresh formal problems. For if the archivolt of the arch across the corner is all on one plane, then its base points will project forwards into space and the niche will overhang part of the enclosed rectangular interior. (See fig. p. 179.)

In the tomb of Sultan Iltutmish we encounter one of the earliest such vaults in India. The archivolt of a pointed arch, based on the Persian prototype, is placed in a vertical plane set diagonally across the corner, so changing the square chamber into an octagonal one. Attempts were made to prevent the round niche from overhanging the corner of the chamber not by placing the reveal of the arch vertically to the archivolt only at the apex of the arch – in contrast to the Persian model – but by making a 45° turn at the base of the arch. In this way the reveal of the arch terminates in the plane of the wall faces. Here, too, the need for clarity of form does not as yet lead to a geometrically well defined solution. The line of intersection of the reveals could have been carried on into the corners of the chamber as an inclined squinch; this would have resulted in a squinch similar to earlier Persian examples. Instead of this an effort was made to repeat the Hindu form of corbelled dome behind the reveal of the arch. This attempt to draw upon Hindu elements to solve a formal problem in Islamic architecture was a failure.

Another outgrowth of solution (b) (see p. 179) is to be found in the mosque of Jamaat Khana, which dates from the fourteenth century. Here the architect, following the model of the Alai Darwaza or Gateway of Ala-ud-din in the Qutb mosque, proceeded from the idea that every kind of bold form should be avoided. The overlappings of the circle (K) and the right angle (W) he avoided by inscribing the round niche into the right angle. As a result of this the base points projected far into the chamber. So he therefore placed only a small round niche in the corner of the chamber and staggered several ogee arches until the squinch obtained the required width. This, however, did not completely solve the problem of the overhang, for these overhangs now appeared smaller in scale and

The so-called 'Turkish triangle' made possible a transition from the cube to an octagon, a 16-sided or a 28-sided polygon

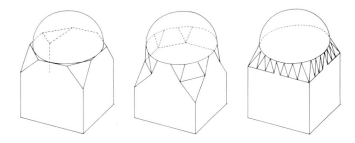

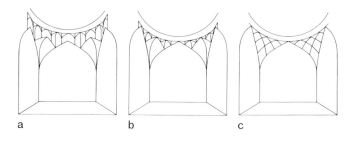

a   b   c

Development of the double row of squinches to a cluster of squinch nets:

a) double row of squinches (Isfahan)
b) superposition of the two rows at one level (Samarkand, Bibi Khanim mosque)
c) developed to form a cluster of squinch nets–the most common form of transition used in Indo-Islamic architecture

less disturbing. Instead of the large interspace (Z) there were now a number of small merlons.

'Turkish triangle'

Another possible way of effecting a transition from the square to the octagon was discovered independently in Turkey and in India. The so-called 'Turkish triangle' was formed by intersecting a pyramid with a cube. The architraves which form the octagon at the springing of the dome rest upon a projecting layer of masonry set diagonally across the corners. In India this triangle was used only to effect a transition between a square and an octagon; in Turkey it was also used to lead over from an octagon to a sixteen-sided polygon, which led to intricate 'draping' –as our Figure illustrates. A fine Indian example of the 'Turkish triangle' may be seen in the mosque at Fathepur Sikri.

Interspaces between ribs (squinch nets)

In Turkey the planes of the triangle were multiplied to make the transition to a sixteen-sided polygon; in

Persia, similarly, a second squinch zone was formed above the first. An example of this variant of simple conical vaulting may be encountered in the great mosque at Isfahan. The disadvantage of this solution is that the small squinches that lead to the sixteen-sided polygon are of a different size from those leading to the octagon. The arches of varying size placed one above the other do indeed give a clear idea of what the architect had in mind, but they are not required for the sake of stability, nor are they required for formal reasons. What therefore can have been more tempting than for some architects to stop placing smaller zones of squinches over the larger ones, and instead to shift them into the interspaces

Diagram showing the eight arches supporting the dome of the Gol Gumbaz, Bijapur

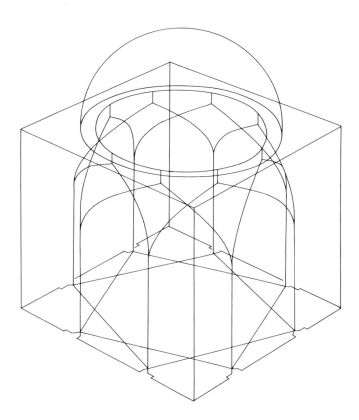

between the latter, and to enlarge them until they were of similar size?

As a result of this change of scale, which was undertaken in order to produce an impression of compactness, those squinches that had previously been small now looked truncated, since only the top of their outline remained (b). (See p. 181.)

Let us sum up. All arches are now of the same shape and size. The eye can follow those that are situated on the axes of the buildings from one base-point to another; of the arches of the larger squinches one can see only the upper half, and of the smaller ones only a quarter. The eye automatically supplies the missing part of the smaller arches, which produces a pattern of overlapping arches. Each panel in this network has the form of a small squinch. In this way are formed the so-called 'clusters of squinch nets' – one of the most popular transitional forms used by Indian architects (c). (See p. 181.)

This development first occurred in Persia; Indian architects adopted the mature form of squinch net and merely made variations upon it. Apart from several special forms (which came about because artisans from the provinces, although familiar with its general idea, did not know anything about its geometric origins), the canon that governed early and simple forms of squinch net was this: each individual arch of the numerous ones in the cluster was in a vertical plane. During the Mughul period the squinch net became increasingly decorative and no longer conformed to this canonical prerequisite.

For the tomb of Sultan Muhammad 'Adil Shah at Bijapur the architect adopted a particularly original arrangement of the squinch net, found in the 'madrasah' at Chargird. In the square ground-plan he inscribed an octagon and then linked pairs of corners, skipping the intermediate one. This gave two squares, set at an angle of 45° to one another, of which none of the sides, however, was parallel to the square formed by the walls of the chamber. Above each side of these inscribed squares he erected an arch and

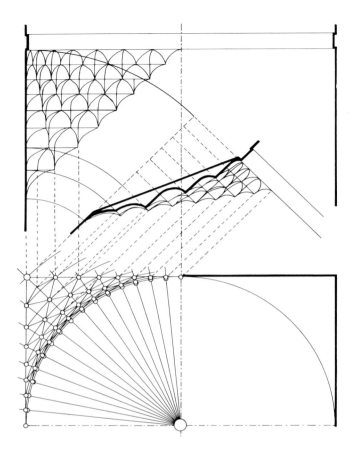

Ground-plan, vertical section, and section of a cluster of stalactites on a conical pendentive (diagrammatic)

backed each panel in the pattern with a squinch. The reason for this ingenious construction was the following: the octagon that was to be crowned with a dome was much smaller than that formed by simply cutting away the corners of a square.

Stalactites

If some architects endeavoured to group together squinches of various sizes in a double zone, others proceeded differently. If one zone leads over to an octagon and a second one to a sixteen-sided polygon, why should not a third, a fourth and yet others be added until one approaches the circular form of the springing of the dome? This evolution, which occurred outside India as well, led to the formation of clusters of niches, called by the Arabs 'mukaranas' and referred to by most architectural historians as 'stalactites'. There is no geometric canon that holds good for all types of such stalactites. Various Islamic countries devised their own ways of constructing them. Since these clusters of niches are generally situated at a great height below the dome and are inaccessible, there are too few accurate photographs of them to enable us to establish their manner of construction. Photographs served as the basis for Rosintal's schematic drawing (modified by La Roche) of a stalactite formation from the tomb of Sultan al-Malik-al-Adil, the Juman-Bai in Cairo, dating from the sixteenth century. It is reproduced here schematically with some alterations by the author. In this case the stalactites cover a spherical pend-

Hybrid form of 'Turkish triangle' and stalactites:

a) exact geometric form
b) variants employed in the mosque at Gulbarga

a   b

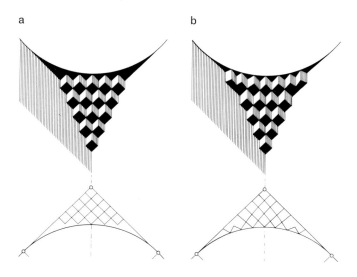

entive. But they also occur within an area of squinches, e.g. in the mosque of the Taj Mahal, or articulate a 'Turkish triangle' as in the sixteenth-century Sher Shah mosque at Delhi.

In constructing stalactites the plaster was not generally applied to a flat base; instead bricks or stones were made to project in such a way that only small niches had to be filled in with stucco. At Gulbarga a plastered structure of this kind, with cubes protruding at various angles, was chosen as a means of effecting the transition from the square panels of the ground-plan to the small cupolas above. In one detail, however, the Gulbarga mosque deviated from the strict geometric form. Of the cubes in the top row only the one in the centre can touch the springing, theoretically speaking; as a result of this the interspaces become ever wider towards the sides (a). Instead of this we have a somewhat distorted cluster of cubes, which lacks any geometric basis but is better adapted to the rounded form of the dome (b). This bold treatment of detail is all the more surprising since the overall design is distinguished by geometric clarity. A small artifice served to bring out the beauty of this cluster of cubes: small apertures were carved in the dome to admit light—these are the only perforated domes in India—so that a ray of sunlight could strike it, producing a contrasting effect of light and shade.

Transport of materials and building sites

The Islamic architects of India were dependent upon those means of transport that had already been in use since ancient times to convey huge monoliths to the site from quarries that were often far distant: namely, ox carts and rafts.

Tavernier reports that during a visit to Agra he encountered on the road a seemingly endless caravan continuously bringing precious white marble from Makrana and Raiwala to the site of the Taj Mahal.

On the other hand, the red sandstone of which most of the Red Fort at Shahjahanabad was built, including the high enclosure wall, comes from Bharatpur, a small town near the River Jumna. It could be shipped upstream by raft and boat to Shahjahanabad.

The transportation of a huge monolith is described in a chronicle from the reign of Firuz Shah (1351–1388), called 'Sham-i-Siraj'. This was an edict pillar originating from the era of the great Buddhist emperor Ashoka, which Firuz Shah discovered in a small village. He had it transported to Delhi, where it was erected on the Kotilal, a multi-storeyed pavilion (for its ground-plan and elevation, see p. 141). 'Khizrabad is situated some 90 'kos' from Delhi, not far from the mountains. When the Sultan visited this district he saw a pillar in the village of Topra and decided to have it taken to Delhi and there erected as a memorial. After thinking how the column could most easily be moved, he gave the order that all the inhabitants of the area, as well as all the foot-soldiers and cavalrymen, should assist in this task. He instructed them to bring with them tools and materials that might be of use in this work. Orders were also issued that bales of wool from the sembal-tree should be brought. Large quantities of this so-called silk-cotton were piled up around the column. When the soil was removed at the base of the column, it tipped over and fell gently on to the bed prepared for it. Gradually the wool was then removed and a few days later the column lay undamaged on the ground. When the foundations were examined a huge ashlar stone was found, which had served as a base. This, too, was dug out.

'Reeds and fresh animal hides were wound around the column so that it should not be damaged. Then a cart was built with 42 wheels, and ropes were fixed to each wheel. By dint of great effort several thousand people lifted the column on to the cart. Now 200 men each pulled on one of the ropes. Only by the simultaneous action of many thousands of people could the cart be moved and drawn to the bank of the Jumna. Here the Sultan was waiting. A number of large boats was already assembled; some of these could carry 5,000 to 7,000 "man" of corn, and the smallest ones at least 2,000 "man".

'With great skill the column was laid on these boats and shipped to Firozabad, where it was transferred to the land and with tremendous effort taken to the palace.

'Then work began on a house near the Jami 'Masjid which was to contain the column. The most able architects and artisans were employed. The building was erected of stone and mortar and consisted of several stepped storeys. As soon as one storey was finished the column was raised to that level. Then the next step was built and the column raised up further. In this way the required height was obtained. Now other artifices were necessary to place it in an upright position. For this stout ropes were brought and winches set up on each step of the six-storeyed building. One end of each rope was tied to the top of the column and the other end to one of the winches, which in turn was firmly anchored. By rotating the winches the column could be raised about half a "gaz". Wooden beams and packs of silk-cotton were laid underneath to prevent it from falling back. Thus the column was raised stage by stage, until after a few days it was upright. Massive beams were erected around it as support, forming a scaffold like a cage. This secured the pillar in an upright position, straight as an arrow, not deviating in the slightest from the vertical. The stone block already mentioned again lay under the column. It measures 32 gaz in height, 8 gaz invisible in the masonry and 24 gaz visible.'

In contrast to Hinduism, in which every part of a temple was fundamentally influenced by symbolic considerations, the teaching of the Prophet Muhammad did not lay down any explicit or implicit precepts governing the construction of buildings. For this reason, just as the mosques of Asia Minor came to bear the imprint of the Byzantine world, so the buildings imported from Persia and erected in India by Islamic rulers could not escape the influence of the Hindu symbolic idiom.

Chronological Table

Buildings in India

500	Mahayana Buddhist caves at Ajanta
650	Rathas at Mahaballipuram (Hindu)
1010	Shiva temple at Tanjore
1200	Quwwat-ul-Islam mosque at Delhi; Qutb Minar
1236	Iltutmish's tomb
1238	Surya temple at Konarak (Hindu)
1268	Keshava temple at Somnathpur (Hindu)
1305	Enlargement of the Quwwat-ul-Islam mosque: Alai Darwaza
1325	Tomb of Ghiyas-ud-din Tughluq I
1367	Jami'Masjid at Gulbarga
1407	Jami'Masjid at Jaunpur
1423	Jami'Masjid at Ahmadabad
1485–1523	Jami'Masjid at Champanir
1500	Man Singh palace in fort at Gwalior
1540	Sher Shah's tomb at Sasaram, Bihar
1565	Humayun's tomb at Delhi
1569–1570	House of Raja Birbal at Fathepur Sikri; Palace of Jodh Bai; Diwan-i-Khas
1570	Jahangiri Mahal in Red Fort at Agra
1612	Akbar's tomb at Sikandra
1615	Ibrahim Rauza, tomb of Sultan Ibrahim II at Bijapur
1620	Datiya palace (Hindu); last enlargements of the temple-city of Madura
1626–1656	Gol Gumbaz, tomb of Sultan Muhammad at Bijapur
1628	I'timad-ud-daula's tomb at Agra
1632–1652	Taj Mahal, tomb of Mumtaz Mahal, at Agra
1644–1658	Jami'Masjid at Delhi
1645	Red Fort at Delhi

Buildings in Near East and Europe

532–563	Santa Sophia at Constantinople
547	San Vitale at Ravenna
706–715	Omayyad mosque at Damascus
715	Qaseir'Amra
785–987	Great Mosque at Cordova
879	Ibn Tulun mosque at Cairo
990–1012	al-Hakim mosque at Cairo
1063–1094	San Marco in Venice
1304–1316	Mausoleum of Sultan Muhammad at Sultaniyeh, Persia
1333–1391	Alhambra, Granada
1440	Palazzo Pitti in Florence (Brunelleschi)
1420–1434	Dome of Florence Cathedral (Brunelleschi)
1547–1561	Dome of St. Peter's in Rome
1550–1556	Mosque of Suleiman I the Magnificent or Suleimaniyeh at Istanbul (Sinan)
1550	Villa Rotonda in Vicenza (Palladio)
1577–1592	Il Redentore in Venice (Palladio)
1631–1710	Versailles

History of Islam in India

991	Sabutigin of Ghazni conquers parts of the Punjab
997–1030	Mahmud of Ghazni conducts forays into India
1052	Chalyukas conquer the empire of the Rashtrakutas
1206	Qutb-ud-din Aibak becomes first sultan in India
1210–1236	Iltutmish
1320–1325	Ghiyas-ud-din Tughluq I founds Tughluq dynasty
1351–1388	Firuz Shah (Tughluq)
1451–1526	Lodi dynasty rules over the sultanate at Delhi
1490	Yusuf, governor and member of the Bahmani dynasty, founds sultanate of Bijapur
1498	Vasco da Gama lands at Calicut
1510	Portuguese conquer Goa
1526	Babur, coming from Kabul, conquers Hindustan and founds Mughul dynasty
1555	Humayun returns with Persian army
1556–1605	Akbar, the Great Mughul
1580	First Jesuit mission at Fathepur Sikri
1599	East India Company receives royal charter
1605–1627	Jahangir, Great Mughul
1612	Shah Jahan, while still Prince Khurram, weds Mumtaz Mahal
1628–1666	Shah Jahan, Great Mughul
1632	Portuguese settlement at Hooghly sacked
1658	Prince Aurangzib imrisons his father Shah Jahan
1658–1707	Aurangzib, Great Mughul
1686	War between English and Mughuls
1739	Nadir Shah of Persia occupies Delhi
1803	British conquer Delhi
1858	Indian Mutiny; banishment of last Mughul
1877	Queen Victoria proclaimed Empress of India

Glossary

Akbar	lit.: 'the Great One'; Great Mughul of India, 1556–1605
bagh	garden
Bundelkhand	region in Northern India
cenotaph	copy of a sarcophagus, left empty
chadar	lit.: 'shawl'; marble water-chute
chaya	eave supported by consoles, on a Hindu façade
Deccan	Central Indian plateau
Din-i-Ilahi	eclectic religion devised by Akbar
Diwan-i-'Am	Public Audience Hall
Diwan-i-Khas	Private Audience Hall
Fathepur	'town of victory'
garbha-griha	cella of Hindu temple
Gol Gumbaz	lit.: 'round dome'; tomb at Bijapur
Great Mughul	title of Islamic emperors in India
Hayat Bakhsh Bagh	'Life-giving Garden'
interspace between ribs (squinch net)	in Indian and Persian buildings, a transitional area between a square area and the circular springing of the dome
Islam	lit.: 'surrender to God'
jali	perforated stone window, lattice
Ka'ba	lit.: 'cube'; sacred black stone at Mecca
khan	ruler, king
liwan	(also 'iwan'): hall in mosque or portal niche in a body of masonry
Mahal	house, palace
Mahtab Bagh	'Moonlight Garden'
mandapa	assembly hall of South Indian temple
mihrab	niche in rear wall of mosque pointing toward Mecca
minar, minaret	turret of mosque
mosque	lit.: 'place of prostration'; Islamic place of worship
mosjid	mosque
mu'azzin	crier who proclaims hours of prayer from minaret
mulla	one learned in Islamic theology and religious studies
Mumtaz Mahal	lit.: 'ornament of the palace'; consort of Shah Jahan
Nur Jahan	lit.: 'light of the world'; consort of Jahangir
Nur Mahal	lit.: 'light of the palace'
pachisi	Indian game played on a board
panch-ratna	lit.: 'five jewels'; design whereby four small domes or kiosks are grouped around a large one
Parsees	followers of the prophet Zoroaster who migrated to India
pietra dura	kind of inlay
qutb	lit.: 'axis'
Qutb-ud-din	lit.: 'axis of faith'; first Sultan of Delhi

Quwwat-ul-Islam	lit.: 'victory of Islam'; mosque in Old Delhi, also known as Qutb mosque
sanyasi	Hindu mendicant monk
Shilpa shastras	Hindu manuals of art and architecture
spoils	parts of a demolished building used in the construction of a new one
stalactites	(also 'mukaranas'): decorative cluster of small niches or squinches
sthapati	Hindu priest-architect
Sufis	members of a mystic movement
Sunnites	followers of Orthodox Islam
swastika	ancient Aryan solar symbol
Taj Mahal	lit.: 'crown of the palace'; tomb of Mumtaz Mahal
tawaf	rite, also pre-Islamic, involving circumambulation of sacred stones
triratna	lit.: 'three jewels'; Buddhist symbolic design

Bibliography

Abu-'l Fazl
The Ain-i Akbari. Delhi, 1965

Ancient India. Bulletins of the Archaeological Survey
of India

Annual Reports of the Archaeological Survey of India,
New Delhi

Babur, Zehir-ed-Din Muhammed
Memoirs. Translated by J. Leyden and W. Erskine,
annotated and revised by Sir Lucas King. London, 1921

Batley, C.
The Design Development of Indian Architecture.
London, 1934; 2nd ed. London, 1940; New York, 1967

Brown, Percy
Indian Architecture: the Islamic Period.
Bombay, 1942; 2nd revised ed. Bombay, 1952

Cambridge History of India. New Delhi – Bombay, 1963

Chaghtai, Muhammad Abdulla
Le Tadj Mahal d'Agra. Editions de la Connaissance,
Brussels, 1938, 1952

Cousens, H.
Bijapur and its Architectural Remains. Archaeological
Survey of India, vol. XXXVII, Imp. Ser., Bombay, 1916

Fanshawe, N. C.
Delhi, Past and Present. London, 1902

Fergusson, J.
History of Indian and Eastern Architecture.
2 vols. London, 1910

Foster, E. W.
Early Travels in India, 1583–1619. London, 1921

Glück, H. and Diez, E.
Die Kunst des Islam. Berlin, 1925

Hankin, E. H.
The Drawing of Geometric Patterns in Saracenic Art.
New Delhi – Calcutta, 1925

Hautecœur, L.
De la trompe aux mukarnas. Gazette des Beaux-Arts,
Paris, July 1931

Havell, E. B.
Handbook to Agra and the Taj. London, 1912;
2nd ed. Calcutta, 1924

Havell, E. B.
Indian Architecture. London, 1913; 2nd ed. London, 1927

Ibn Batuta
The Travels of Ibn Battuta. Translated from the Arabic
text, edited by C. Defrémery and B. R. Sanguinetti,
by H. A. R. Gibb. Cambridge, 1958

Langenegger, F.
Die Baukunst des Iraq (heutiges Babylonien)…
Diss. Dresden, 1911

La Roche, E.
Indische Baukunst. Munich, 1921

Le Bon, G.
Les monuments de l'Inde… Paris, 1893

Mžik, Hans von
Die Reise des Arabers Ibn Batuta durch Indien und China.
Hamburg, 1911

Pascha, F.
Die Baukunst des Islam. (Handbuch der Architektur.)
Darmstadt, 1887

Reuther, O.
Indische Paläste und Wohnhäuser. Berlin, 1925

Rosintal, J.
Pendentifs, trompes et stalactites dans l'architecture
orientale. Paris, 1928

Rosintal, J.
Le réseau. Paris, 1937

Smith, E. W.
Mughal Architecture of Fathepur Sikri. Archaeological
Survey of India. New Imperial Series of Reports, vol. 18.
Allahabad, 1896

Smith, Vincent A.
A History of Fine Art in India and Ceylon. Bombay, 1962

Tavernier, J.B.
Travels in India. London, 1925

Villiers-Stuart, C.M.
Gardens of the Great Mughals. London, 1913

Wetzel, F.
Islamische Grabbauten in Indien aus der Zeit der Soldaten-
kaiser, 1320–1540. Leipzig, 1918

Text references

[1] R.C. Majumdar, An Advanced History of India, London, 1960, p. 332

[2] Cambridge History of India, vol. IV, Mughul Period, Cambridge, 1937, p. 14

[3] E.B. Havell, Agra and the Taj, Calcutta, 1924, pp. 21f.

[4] J.-B. Tavernier, Travels in India, London, 1925, p. 274

[5] Early Travels in India, Edited by E.W. Foster, London, 1921, pp. 155–6

[6] Memoirs of Jahangir, Translated by A. Rogers, Edited by H. Beveridge, London, 1909, vol. I, pp. 280, 368

[7] Memoirs of Zehir-ed-Din Muhammed Babur, Translated by J. Leyden and W. Erskine, London, 1921, vol. II, pp. 206, 242

[8] Ibid., vol. I, p. 227

[9] Ibid., vol. II, p. 135

[10] C.M. Villiers-Stuart, Gardens of the Great Mughals, London, 1913, p. 190

[11] Ibid., p. 66

[12] Early Travels in India, Edited by E.W. Foster, London, 1921, pp. 17–18

[13] The Ain I Akbari by Abul Fazl'Allami, Translated by H. Blackmann, vol. I, Calcutta, 1873, pp. 222f.

[14] Ibid., pp. 223f.

A simplified spelling has been adopted for names in Oriental languages.

Acknowledgements

The references in the figures and diagrams are as follows (a = above; b = below; r = right; l = left):

Archaeological Survey of India: 13/14, 37, 38, 40, 46, 56 b, 57/58, 78, 88, 89 r, 89 l, 97/98, 129, 130, 147/148, 176

Batley, C.: 50

Brown, P.: 44, 45, 47, 48, 51 l, 87, 180, 181 r

Fergusson, J.: 138, 171 l

Fischer, K. and Snigula, F.: 178 r

Hankin, E.H.: 143 l, 143 r, 144 a, 144 b, 145 l, 145 r, 146

Herdeg, K.: 132, 133

La Roche, E.: 42, 55, 81, 84, 96, 141 r, 172, 182

Reuther, O.: 77, 141 l

Rosintal, J.: 180 r

Russian Imperial Archaeological Society: 83

Villiers-Stuart, M.: 91, 94 l, 94 r, 95

Volwahsen, A.: 41, 46, 53, 56 a, 82, 85 a, 85 b, 137 a, 137 b, 139, 171 r, 178 l, 179 l, 179 r, 181 l, 183

Wetzel, F.: 51 r, 52